"the very practice of reading will have a purifying effect upon your mind and heart. Let nothing take the place of this daily exercise."

Billy Graham

A friend of mine wrote this. I hope you enjoy your Daily Acts.

♡, Brandon

ENDORSEMENTS FOR DAILY ACTS

"In DAILY ACTS, Lalla Lee Campsen shares a systematic approach to prayer she developed over more than twenty years leading prayer and Bible study groups. Built upon the firm foundation of Scripture, DAILY ACTS is a means of grace that will enrich your prayer life and deepen your relationship with the God who made us."

—Tim Scott
United States Senator

"I am personally helped to pray by the faithful, biblical prayers of fellow believers, especially when they are written down. Such prayers by John Calvin, Augustin Marlorat, Matthew Henry, Isaac Watts, C.H. Spurgeon, F.B. Meyer, Tim Keller, and others can be found on about half a shelf of small books of scriptural prayer, immediately to my right hand as I write this. I have now added the name of Lalla Lee Campsen to the list of godly people who help me in prayer.

Her book DAILY ACTS blessed me as I read and used it in manuscript form, and now has joined my little shelf of books to help me come to the Father, through the Son, by the Spirit, with the Scriptures. Her useful and encouraging book is organized in five sections, offering different ways of arranging our daily intercession: biblical topical prayers, organized alphabetically; prayers arranged around the fruits of the Spirit; prayers for particular groups of people; thematic and topical prayers (for instance, using the Lord's Prayer or the Golden Rule); and prayers for the holidays.

I am deeply thankful for her labors in preparing the book, but especially for her example in prayer. May the Lord use this book to help us offer up our desires unto God, for things agreeable to his will, in the name of Christ, with confession of our sins, and thankful acknowledgment of his mercies."

—Ligon Duncan
Chancellor and CEO, Reformed Theological Seminary

"Most of us want to grow our prayer lives, but don't know where to begin. Lalla Lee has created a wonderful resource to help develop a robust and thriving prayer life. Her new book, DAILY ACTS, will help you pray, while it teaches you how to pray. With the Bible as the foundation for each topic, this book will encourage you to pray in deeper and richer ways—I highly recommend it!"

—*Melissa Kruger*
Director of Women's Initiatives for The Gospel Coalition

"Lalla Lee Campsen has made me wish I had been given this book fifty years ago! It is a marvelous resource that will profoundly implement a routine of real, strong, and courageous prayer. I foresee an army of prayer warriors emerging in the days to come, changed and equipped by this book, and what an influence that will have on this hurting world of ours. I fully endorse and recommend this book. But a warning: don't read it unless you are willing for your prayer life to change dramatically. You have been warned."

—*Derek W. H. Thomas*
Senior Minister, First Presbyterian Church, Columbia. SC
Teaching Fellow, Ligonier Ministries
Chancellor's Professor, Reformed Theological Seminary

"Most books I read make a deposit 'in' me. I glean new information or develop a better understanding and then move to the next book. DAILY ACTS, however, was different. Not that I didn't receive valuable insights from it. I did. The book was biblical, theological, devotional, and very practical. DAILY ACTS went beyond making a deposit 'in' me. It drew something 'out' of me, a deeper longing to know Christ more intimately and His Word more thoroughly. Lalla Lee Campsen has spent years on her knees and it shows."

—*Bill Jones*
Chancellor, Columbia International University

"Praying God's Word through a structured (ACTS) and alphabetical format was a new and seemingly limiting way to pray for me, but it proved to be quite the opposite. Praying this way has blown open my prayer life! Guided by His very words from Scripture (instead of my own fears and needs), I am bathed in comfort and confidence that He hears and answers our prayers."

—*Mary Tutterow*
Author of *The Heart of the Caregiver* Bible study series.

"DAILY ACTS is an easy to use, spirit-filled prayer guide for all ages. This marvelous book integrates biblical references and special types of prayers with topics people often think about.

God called Lalla Lee Campsen to develop this unique prayer book. She has poured her heart and soul into this invaluable resource that offers four approaches to prayer, counsel for godly living, and God's plan for eternal security through Jesus Christ. The four approaches to prayer are summarized in the acronym ACTS: Adoration, Confession, Thanksgiving, and Supplication.

Christ's followers as well as non-believers will benefit greatly from this resource with fifty-two chapters, one for each week of the year. Each chapter will be extremely helpful for prayer offerings and devotionals.

Of special significance, this book repeatedly points to the importance that before one can walk with the Lord, they must first accept Jesus Christ as Savior and Lord. I especially liked the easy method Lalla Lee offers for sharing the gospel using the ABC's. I plan to use this helpful guide in sharing the 'Good News.'

I have had the pleasure of serving as president and professor of Charleston Southern University, a distinctively Christian university. Mr. and Mrs. W. Norris Lightsey, Lalla Lee's grandparents, were founders of this university. I feel sure that her grandparents are looking down and thanking the Lord for Lalla Lee's calling and preparation of this book. I wholeheartedly recommend DAILY ACTS as an exceptional prayer guide."

—*Jairy Hunter*
President Emeritus, Charleston Southern University

"Every chef has a test kitchen to try out the recipes before they serve their special guests at a dinner party. I have been blessed to be a part of Lalla Lee's DAILY ACTS test group. For years, we have met weekly together to pray for our children, families, friends, and this next generation worldwide. Following her example found in DAILY ACTS, we have prayed week by week from A-Z. How thankful I am to invite you to come join us as you read through DAILY ACTS! 'Oh, taste and see that the Lord is good, blessed is the one who trusts in Him.' This will be a book you will want to share with all and invite them saying 'Come, see, and pray with me.'"

—*Michaelene Sanders*
Online Trainer, Bible Study Fellowship International

"Witnessing the evolution of DAILY ACTS from inception to final polish, as I was fortunate to do, it was plain early on that the concept, method, and execution was the result of vigilance and effort, of focus and determination, patience and study, and over a span of some twenty years. So, while we must call this a first book, and though Lalla Lee Campsen will be considered a new author, this is not the work of a novice, but that of a veteran writer and thinker, a woman not only in possession of all the right instincts, but with the talent and grace to give them speech."

—*David Teems*
Author of *Majestie: The King Behind the King James Bible;*
Tyndale: The Man Who Gave God and English Voice

"Congratulations on an excellent book! It is heartfelt and created with love – of the Lord and others. I know this book will help others in their prayer life now and for generations to come. What a feat!"

—*Jenny Sanford McKay*
Former First Lady of South Carolina
Author, *Staying True*

DAILY ACTS

A YEARLY GUIDE TO
PRAYER AND PRAISE

LALLA LEE CAMPSEN

J. Westin Books
100 Missionary Ridge
Birmingham, AL 35242
An imprint of Iron Stream Media
IronStreamMedia.com

Iron Stream Media serves its authors as they express their views, which may not express the views of the publisher.

Library of Congress Cataloging-in-Publication Data 2020918641

Unless otherwise indicated, all Scripture quotations are from the NIV version.

Unless stated as ESV, All the verses are from NIV ©1973,1978,1984 by International Bible Society. Use by permission of Zondervan Publishing House. Used by permission. All rights reserved.

Find Us Faithful – (CMG Song# 3529)—Copyright © 1987 Birdwing Music (ASCAP) Jonathan Mark Music (ASCAP) (adm. at CapitolCMGPublishing.com) All rights reserved. Used by permission.

Paperback ISBN-13: 978-1-56309-469-9
Hardback ISBN-13: 978-1-56309-480-4
eBook ISBN: 978-1-56309-472-9

2 3 4 5 6—24 23 22 21 20

To George and Boyce, my beloved sons

As a young teenager, I prayed for the children God might one day graciously give me. The Lord answered my prayer exceedingly, abundantly, more than anything I dreamed or imagined by giving you to me. What a great privilege and blessing it is to be your mom and pray for you! You are precious in my sight. I cherish the friendship we now share. This book is dedicated to you, God's gracious gifts to me. I love you dearly!

ACKNOWLEDGMENTS

In the preface of his book THE DIVINE CONQUEST, A.W. Tozer wrote, "The only book that should be written is one that flows up from the heart, forced out by inward pressure." I acknowledge inward promptings of the Holy Spirit in writing this book, but also I acknowledge the encouragement of friends who provided the outward pressure to write DAILY ACTS.

To Nancy Drake, Michaelene Sanders, and Mary Tutterow. Over the span of many years, we have prayed either in person or in spirit the prayers contained in this book. At your imploring, I compiled some of our prayers. To you, I owe a debt of gratitude for your faithfulness to prayer and encouragement to write.

To Paul Shepherd. Like my Good Shepherd who sought me, his lost sheep, you, my literary agent, sought my work. While wandering in the writing process, you steered me in the right direction. To you, I owe a debt of gratitude for your guidance and direction.

To David Teems. Through your years of experience as a best selling author, musician, songwriter, and editor, you coached me well and helped me make appropriate edits to this manuscript. Thank you for helping me to make necessary amendments and revisions. To you, I owe a debt of gratitude for your patience with me, a first time author.

To Chip, my devoted husband. As a college student, one of the first invitations I received from you was to attend your Sunday school class. With depth and conviction you taught and spurred me on in my faith. From the start, I have respected your mind and appreciated your passion for God and his Word. Your gift of teaching has deeply enriched my biblical understanding. To you, I owe a debt of gratitude for the years of love, dedication, and support you have given me, especially through this writing project. Thank you for the hours spent reading, praying, and making appropriate suggestions to enhance this book.

Of course, my biggest debt of gratitude is to my Heavenly Father for loving me enough to adopt me as his own through his Son's propitiation and sending his Holy Spirit as my Advocate. To God be all the glory, honor and praise!

O God, I say, "to you I pray"
And yet I "fib" 'bout every day
Cause I never do the things I should
Or even those I wish I could.

Oh! How my conscience gnaws at me
When it's things for Christ I need to be
Concerned with now – and not my own
Trivia that has my mind all blown.

You never let me down at all
You're always there, whene'er I call
The answers that you give to me
So far exceed the dreams I see.

I know, dear Lord, that you are there
Ever listening to each prayer
And so please let me stop today
To give you time – I need to pray.

Written 7 February 1984 by my precious mother
Nell Lightsey Laffitte
(1930-1998)

My heart I offer to you, O Lord, promptly and sincerely.
—John Calvin

TABLE OF CONTENTS

MY STORY xvii

HOW TO USE THIS BOOK xix

I. PRAYERS AND PRAISE FROM A TO Z

  1 Abide In Christ. 25

  2 Be Blameless. 31

  3 Clothed In Compassion 37

  4 Delight In The Lord 43

  5 Enlightened 47

  6 Friendship 51

  7 Good And Generous 55

  8 Holy 61

  9 Imitator Of God 67

10 Just 71

11 Knowledgeable. 77

12 Let Your Light Shine. 83

13 Merciful 89

14 No One Take You Captive 95

15 Obedient 101

16 Perseverance 105

17 Quiet Life 111

18 Resolved 115

19 Spirit Filled. 121

20 Trust 125

21 Undivided Heart 129

22 Hear Your Voice 133

23 Walk In Your Way 137

24 Excel In Everything 143

25 Yearn For The Lord 147

26 Zeal For The Lord 151

II. PRAYERS FOR THE FRUIT OF THE HOLY SPIRIT

27 Love 157

28 Joy 161

29 Peace 165

30 Patience 169

31 Kindness 173

32 Goodness 177

33 Faithfulness 181

34 Gentleness 185

35 Self-Control 191

III. PRAYERS FOR PARTICULAR PEOPLE

36 Family And Friends 197

37 Missionaries And Ministries 201

38 Authority 205

39 Weak And Sick 211

40 The Next Generation 215

IV. PRAYERS BY TOPIC

41 Marks Of A Christian 221

42 Attitude 225

43 Overcoming Evil With Good 229

44 Scriptural Prayer For Difficult Times 233

45 The Greatest Commandment 237

46 The Golden Rule 241

47 The Lord's Prayer .245

48 Salvation 249

V. PRAYERS FOR THE HOLIDAYS

49 New Year 257

50 Easter 261

51 Thanksgiving 267

52 Christmas 271

BENEDICTION 277

BIBLIOGRAPHY 279

MY STORY

This story is not mine alone. It is the story of hundreds of others who have prayed alongside me. Some I have known, some I have never met, but all have joined me in praying the prayers contained in this book.

My story began over twenty years ago upon hearing a *Focus on the Family* broadcast featuring Fern Nichols, the founder of *Moms in Prayer.* "The burden to intercede for my boys was so overwhelming," Fern said, "that I could not bear it alone. I asked God to give me another mom who felt the same burden and who was willing to pray with me concerning our children and their school." Her message resonated with me and the Lord impressed upon my heart the desire to "go and do likewise." I prayed and the Lord gave.

In 1998, while in my car at a movie theater parking lot, a mother and I met to pray for our elementary age children. Over the years, the size of the prayer group has expanded and contracted. The weekly hour of prayer has continued through my children's college careers and into their adult lives.

Desiring the prayer time to be focused, I compiled weekly scriptural prayer sheets. I needed this structure because I found myself in the rut John Piper has described:

> *If I try to pray for people or events without having the Word in front of me guiding my prayers, then several negative things happen. One is that I tend to be very repetitive ... I just pray the same things all the time. Another negative thing is that my mind tends to wander.*[1]

This book is a compilation of prayer sheets that have been used not only by my group, but also by prayer warriors across the nation. And it is not only for parents, but also for anyone who desires a more focused time of prayer, individually or in a group setting.

---

[1] John Piper, "Should I Use the Bible When I Pray?" Article in *desiringgod.org.*, September 28, 2007.

Question 98 of the *Westminster Shorter Catechism* asks, "What is prayer?" The answer: "Prayer is the offering up of our desires unto God for things agreeable to his will, in the name of Christ, with the confession of our sins and thankful acknowledgement of his mercies." Prayer, so described, can be summarized in the acronym ACTS—Adoration, Confession, Thanksgiving, and Supplication. The prayers contained in this book are the word of God composed with that acronym in mind.

With fifty-two chapters, one for each week of the year, I encourage you to meditate and pray every day, through one chapter a week. Choose one verse per week and memorize it, in order to "store up God's word in your hearts so that you will not sin against him."[2]

My prayer is that DAILY ACTS will be a helpful guide as you "pour your heart out like water in the presence of the LORD."[3]

---

[2] PSALM 119:11.

[3] LAMENTATIONS 2:19.

How to Use this Book & Pray the ACTS format

Using ACTS (Adoration, Confession, Thanksgiving, Supplication) as a guide, each section focuses on a particular type of prayer.

PRAYERS OF ADORATION

Acknowledge who God is. Take time to "gaze upon the beauty of the LORD,"[1] to "ascribe to the LORD the glory due his Name,"[2] to focus upon him—his names, his titles, his attributes, his providence.

PRAYERS OF CONFESSION

Confess you are a sinner in desperate need of the Savior's grace. Specifically, name your sins of omission and commission. Be transparent. The Bible states, "your iniquities have made a separation between you and your God, and your sins have hidden his face from you so that he does not hear."[3] It also says, "If we cherish or regard iniquity in our hearts, the Lord will not hear us."[4] Therefore, we "confess our sins to each other and pray for each other that we may be healed."[5]

PRAYERS OF THANKSGIVING

Express gratitude and acknowledgment of what God has done. Declare God's goodness, especially for answered prayers. Note the difference between adoration and thanksgiving. Adoration focuses on God. Thanksgiving focuses on what he has done.

---

[1] PSALM 27:4.

[2] PSALM 29:2.

[3] ISAIAH 59:2.

[4] PSALM 66:18.

[5] JAMES 5:16.

Offer your requests in accordance with God's Word and his will. Scripture states, "Humble yourselves, therefore, under God's mighty hand, that he may lift you up in due time. Cast all your anxiety on him because he cares for you." (1 PETER 5:6). Therefore, let your requests be made known to God and intercede on behalf of those the Lord has placed upon your heart.

The Adoration section in chapters 1–26 focuses upon the person of God—his names, titles, and attributes beginning with a letter of the alphabet. This systematic approach highlights a multitude of God's characteristics for which he is to be praised.

Recalling the names of God is important. Each name reveals something specific about his nature. By studying and knowing God's names and their meanings, one can grow in relationship with him. In their book, NAME ABOVE ALL NAMES, Alistair Begg & Sinclair B. Ferguson state the following:

Jesus Christ has been given the name above all names. The names assigned him begin in Genesis and end in Revelation. Taken together they express the incomparable character of Jesus Christ, our Savior and Lord. Reflecting on them better prepares us to respond to the exhortations of Scripture, to focus our gaze upon him, and to meditate on how great he is.[6]

In chapters 1–26, the Supplication section highlights key words in Scripture associated with a letter of the alphabet. Fill in the blank with the names of those for whom you desire to pray. Consider saying a prayer for people whose first or last name begins with that letter. The idea is to pray for people whom you might not ordinarily pray.

The focus of prayer in chapters 27–35 is on God's work in our lives through the power of the Holy Spirit as seen in the Fruit of the

[6] Alistair Begg & Sinclair B. Ferguson, NAME ABOVE ALL NAMES (CROSSWAY, 2013), 15.

Spirit. In chapters 36–40, the focus is on particular people groups. Chapters 41–52 focus on topical and thematic prayers.

The prayers contained in this guide are to be prayed conversationally, as prayer is never alone. It is a dialogue that engages at least two parties—you and God; or you, God, and others. Regardless who is party to the conversation, conscientiously place your heart and mind in the presence of God. Begin the dialogue by reading the Scriptures aloud. Pause and pray after each section. Add your own adorations, confessions, thanksgiving, and supplications. Ask the Holy Spirit to guide your time of prayer and to intercede on your behalf.[7]

At the end of each ACTS section is a reflection—some personal, some doctrinal. The intent is to "proclaim to you the testimony about God."[8] Consider journaling your thoughts and prayers; keep track of those people and things for which you have prayed. In the years to come, you will be able to look back and "tell the next generation the praiseworthy deeds of the LORD, his power, and the wonders he has done."[9]

I pray this guide will cause you to draw near to God[10] in such a way that your love for him will "abound more and more in knowledge and depth of insight."[11] I pray you see the glory and the majesty of God on every page, so that your desire to be in his presence increases as you walk and talk with him. It is my hope that prayers of adoration, confession, thanksgiving, and supplication will be part of your DAILY ACTS.

---

[7] ROMANS 8:26–27.

[8] 1 CORINTHIANS 2:1–5.

[9] PSALM 78:4.

[10] JAMES 4:8 ESV.

[11] PHILIPPIANS 1:9–10.

SECTION I

PRAYERS AND PRAISE
FROM A TO Z

CHAPTER 1

ABIDE IN CHRIST

ADORATION

Praise God for his names, titles, and attributes that begin with *A*.

Praise God! He is *awesome* above all.

> Let the heavens praise your wonders, O LORD, your faithfulness in the assembly of the holy ones! For who in the skies can be compared to the LORD? Who among the heavenly beings is like the LORD, a God greatly to be feared in the council of the holy ones, and awesome above all who are around him?
> —PSALM 89:5–7 ESV

Praise God! He is the *Alpha* and the Omega, the *Almighty.*

> "I am the Alpha and the Omega," says the Lord God, "who is, and who was, and who is to come, the Almighty."
> —REVELATIONS 1:8

> I am God Almighty.
> —GENESIS 17:1

Praise God! He is the *Ancient of Days.*

> As I looked, thrones were set in place, and the Ancient of Days (Almighty God) took his seat. His clothing was as white as snow; the hair of his head was like pure wool. His throne was flaming with fire and its wheels were all ablaze.
> —DANIEL 7:9

Praise God! He is the *author* of our faith.

> Let us fix our eyes on Jesus, the author and perfecter of our faith.
> —HEBREWS 12:2

Praise God! He is the *anchor* of our souls.

> We have this hope as an anchor for the soul, firm and secure.
> —HEBREWS 6:19

Praise God! He is our *Advocate*.

> But the Advocate, the Holy Spirit, whom the Father will send in my name, will teach you all things and will remind you of everything I have said to you.
> —JOHN 14:26

Praise God! We are his *adopted* children. He is our *Abba Father*.

> You have received the Spirit of adoption as sons, by whom we cry, "Abba! Father!"
> —ROMANS 8:15 ESV

PAUSE AND ADORE HIM.

CONFESSION

> Against you, you only, have I sinned and done what is evil in your sight, so that you may be justified in your words and blameless in your judgment.
> —PSALM 51:4 ESV

> Help us, O God of our salvation, for the glory of your name; deliver us, and atone for our sins, for your name's sake!
> —PSALM 79:9 ESV

> For we have all have sinned and fall short of the glory of God.
> —ROMANS 3:23

PAUSE AND CONFESS YOUR SINS.

THANKSGIVING

I want you to know that the Son of Man has authority on earth to forgive sins.
—MATTHEW 9:6

We have been "justified freely by his grace through the redemption that came by Christ Jesus. God presented him as a sacrifice of atonement, through faith in his blood. He did this to demonstrate his justice, because in his forbearance he had left the sins committed beforehand unpunished—he did it to demonstrate his justice at the present time, so as to be just and the one who justifies those who have faith in Jesus." —ROMANS 3:24–26

Now to him who is able to keep you from stumbling and to present you blameless before the presence of his glory with great joy, to the only God, our Savior, through Jesus Christ our Lord, be glory, majesty, dominion and authority, before all time now and forever. Amen.
—JUDE 24–25 ESV

PAUSE AND THANK HIM.

SUPPLICATION

Abba Father, my heart's desire is that _____ will receive the Spirit of adoption and be God's child, an heir of God and co-heir with Christ (ROMANS 8:15–16 ESV).

I pray _____ will abide in you and you in him/her, that _____ will bear much fruit, and know that apart from you, he/she can do nothing (JOHN 15:5).

May _____ know that "He who dwells in the shelter of the Most High will abide in the shadow of the Almighty" (PSALM 91:1 ESV).

PRAY FOR THOSE WHOSE NAME BEGINS WITH *A*.

REFLECTION

This week's ACTS included prayers and praises about continually abiding in our Abba Father who adopted us, making us part of his family. Our adoption grants privileges inherent to a child. It is distinct from our regeneration and justification.

Wayne Grudem, in his book SYSTEMATIC THEOLOGY: AN INTRODUCTION TO BIBLICAL DOCTRINE, explains it this way: "Regeneration has to do with our spiritual life within. Justification has to do with our standing before God's law. But our adoption has to do with our relationship with God as our Father, and in adoption we are given many of the greatest blessings that we will know for all eternity."[1]

In John 15, Jesus uses a garden metaphor to illustrate how we, the branch, have been grafted or adopted into Christ, the vine. Jesus describes the organic relationship between his Father, the Master Gardener; himself, the vine; and his disciples, the branches. By using the word "abide" ten times in the first seventeen verses, Jesus stresses the importance of the branch's remaining connected to the vine. Connectivity to our Triune God is maintained through the study of God's word, mediation, and prayer. Jesus' illustration beautifully portrays the dependent nature of we, the branch, upon Christ, the vine, for all necessary nutrients needed to grow and bear spiritual fruit.

All gardeners know, "Gardens are not made by singing 'Oh, how beautiful' and sitting in the shade."[2] Fruit-producing gardens involve planning and preparation along with planting and pruning. They require time, hard work, and attentiveness to flourish, bloom, and grow.

---

[1] Wayne Grudem, SYSTEMATIC THEOLOGY: AN INTRODUCTION TO BIBLICAL DOCTRINE, (Zondervan, 1994), 739.

[2] Rudyard Kipling, C. R. L. Fletcher, "The Glory of the Garden," A SCHOOL HISTORY OF ENGLAND, (London: Clarendon Press, 1911).

Beloved branch, are you being intentional in your effort to cultivate spiritual fruit in your life? Do the work necessary to "be like a well-watered garden, like a spring whose waters never fail."[3] Daily stay connected with the Master Gardener through reading the Word, worship and prayer. Find comfort in knowing that, "the Lord will guide you always; he will satisfy your needs in a sun-scorched land and will strengthen your frame"[4] as you abide in him.

---

[3] Isaiah 58:11.

[4] Ibid.

CHAPTER 2

BE BLAMELESS

ADORATION

Praise God for his names, titles, and attributes that begin with **B**.

Praise God! He is the *Beginning*.

> I am the Alpha and the Omega, the First and the Last, the Beginning and the End.
> —REVELATION 22:13

Praise God! He is *before all things*.

> He is before all things, and in him all things hold together.
> —COLOSSIANS 1:17

Praise God! He is our *bread*.

> I am the living bread that came down from heaven. Whoever eats of this bread will live forever. This bread is my flesh, which I will give for the life of the world.
> —JOHN 6:51

> I am the bread of life. Whoever comes to me will never go hungry, and whoever believes in me will never be thirsty.
> —JOHN 6:35

> For the bread of God is he who comes down from heaven and gives life to the world.
> —JOHN 6:33

Praise God! He is our *builder*.

> God is the builder of everything.
> —HEBREWS 3:4; 11:10

Praise God! He is the *"balm* of Gilead."

> Is there no balm in Gilead; is there no physician there?
> —JEREMIAH 8:22

Praise God! He is our *Banner.*

> Moses built an altar and called it The LORD is my Banner.
> —EXODUS 17:15

Praise God! He is the *beautiful branch.*

> The Branch of the LORD will be beautiful and glorious.
> —ISAIAH 4:2

Praise God! He makes all things *beautiful.*

> He has made everything beautiful in its time. He has also set
> eternity in the hearts of men; yet they cannot fathom what
> God has done from beginning to end.
> —ECCLESIASTES 3:11

Praise God! He is our *bridegroom.*

> Here comes the bridegroom! Come out to meet him!
> —MATTHEW 25:6

PAUSE AND ADORE HIM.

CONFESSION

> Although our sins testify against us, O LORD, do something for
> the sake of your name. For our backsliding is great; we have
> sinned against you.
> —JEREMIAH 14:7

PAUSE AND CONFESS YOUR SINS.

THANKSGIVING

Because of the LORD's great love, we are not consumed, for his compassions never fail. They are new every morning; great is your faithfulness.
—LAMENTATIONS 3:22–23

PAUSE AND THANK HIM.

SUPPLICATION

Blessed Redeemer, beautiful Savior, I pray that _____ will "be an imitator of God, therefore, as a dearly loved child, that he/she will live a life of love" (EPHESIANS 5:1).

May _____ "make every effort to be found spotless, blameless, and at peace with you" (2 PETER 3:14).

I pray for "the blessing of the LORD be upon _____ " (PSALM 129:8).

PRAY FOR THOSE WHOSE NAME BEGINS WITH **B**.

REFLECTION

"He is before all things, and in him all things hold together."[1] What does that mean? It means the Christian Godhead, one God in three persons, Father, Son, and Holy Spirit, existed before creation. This biblical teaching of the pre-existence of Christ is recorded in the first chapter of JOHN.[2] It means there was never a time when Jesus Christ, the Son of God, was not. "He was with God in the

---

[1] COLOSSIANS 1:17.

[2] JOHN 1:1–18.

beginning."[3] Therefore, as the Scripture confirms, he is "before all things."[4]

Doctrinally known as God's providence, God is holding all things together[5] by actively controlling, nourishing, preserving, protecting, maintaining, and governing everything that exists. "Though the term *providence* is not found in Scripture, it has been traditionally used to summarize God's ongoing relationship to his creation."[6] God's providence means the Triune God is dynamically involved "sustaining all things by his powerful word."[7]

It is worth noting the distinction between God's sovereignty and providence. God's sovereignty is "God's exercise of power over his creation."[8] God's providence is his continual involvement "with all created things in such a way that he (1) keeps them existing and maintaining the properties with which he created them; (2) cooperates with created things in every action, directing their distinctive properties to cause them to act as they do; and (3) directs them to fulfill his purposes."[9]

There have been times when I do not feel like God is powerfully in control, that life is a mess. At those times, I have found it helpful to remember a slogan I was taught as a teenager—"Fact! Faith! Feeling!" The words were inscribed upon a train with the locomotive engine as "Fact," fueled by the coal car of "Faith," and followed by the caboose, "Feeling." Ordering the train cars aright—Fact, Faith, Feeling—is essential to sustainability; otherwise, the train derails.

[3] JOHN 1:2.

[4] COLOSSIANS 1:17.

[5] Ibid.

[6] Wayne Grudem, SYSTEMATIC THEOLOGY, AN INTRODUCTION TO BIBLICAL DOCTRINE, (Zondervan 1994), 315.

[7] HEBREWS 1:3.

[8] Wayne Grudem, SYSTEMATIC THEOLOGY, AN INTRODUCTION TO BIBLICAL DOCTRINE, (Zondervan 1994), 1255.

[9] Wayne Grudem, SYSTEMATIC THEOLOGY, AN INTRODUCTION TO BIBLICAL DOCTRINE, (Zondervan 1994), 1252.

When your life seems to be a train wreck, pull out the manual of God's Word. Put your trust in the fact that God, the engineer and conductor, is in control, holding all things together. His Spirit and the Word will fuel your faith. The feelings of peace and rest will follow as you trust in God's sovereign and sustaining power.

CHAPTER 3

CLOTHED IN COMPASSION

ADORATION

Praise God for his names, titles, and attributes that begin with *C*.

Praise God! He is our *Creator*.

> Do you not know? Have you not heard? The Lord is the everlasting God, the Creator of the ends of the earth. He will not grow tried or weary, and His understanding no one can fathom.
> —ISAIAH 40:28

Praise God! He is our *cornerstone.*

> You are no longer foreigners and aliens, but fellow citizens with God's people and members of God's household, built on the foundation of the apostles and prophets, with Christ Jesus himself as the cornerstone. In him the whole building is joined together and rises to become a holy temple in the Lord. And in him you too are being built together into a dwelling in which God lives by his Spirit.
> —EPHESIANS 2:19–22

> Behold, I am the one who has laid as a foundation in Zion, a stone, a tested stone, a precious cornerstone, of a sure foundation.
> —ISAIAH 28:16 ESV

Praise God! He is the One who does not *change.*

> God is not man, that he should lie, or a son of man, that he should change his mind. Has he said, and will he not do it? Or has he spoken, and will he not fulfill it?
> —NUMBERS 23:19 ESV

Praise God! He is our *Wonderful Counselor.*

> And he will be called Wonderful Counselor, Mighty God, Everlasting Father, Prince of Peace.
> —Isaiah 9:6

Praise God! He is *compassionate.*

> Because of the Lord's great love we are not consumed, for his compassions never fail. They are new every morning; great is your faithfulness.
> —Lamentations 3:22–23

Praise God! He is *close.*

> The Lord is close to the brokenhearted and saves the crushed in spirit.
> —Psalm 34:18

Praise God! He is the One who *comforts.*

> The Lord comforts his people.
> —Isaiah 49:13

Praise God! He is *caring.*

> Cast all your anxieties on him, because he cares for you.
> —1 Peter 5:7

Praise God the Father! Praise God the Son, Jesus *Christ*!

> You are the Christ, the Son of the living God.
> —Matthew 16:16

PAUSE AND ADORE HIM.

CONFESSION

We continue to sin against your ways. All of us have become like one who is unclean, and all our righteous acts are like filthy rags. We waste away because of our sins.
—ISAIAH 64:5–7

Therefore, confess your sins to each other and pray for each other so that you many be healed. The prayer of a righteous man is powerful and effective.
—JAMES 5:16

PAUSE AND CONFESS YOUR SINS.

THANKSGIVING

Yet he, being compassionate, atoned for their iniquity and did not destroy them; he restrained his anger often and did not stir up all his wrath.
—PSALM 78:38 ESV

Open to me the gates of righteousness, that I may enter through them and give thanks to the LORD. This is the gate of the LORD; the righteous shall enter through it. I thank you that you have answered me and have become my salvation. The stone that the builders rejected has become the cornerstone. This is the LORD's doing; it is marvelous in our eyes. This is the day that the LORD has made; let us rejoice and be glad in it.
—PSALM 118:19–24 ESV

PAUSE AND THANK HIM.

SUPPLICATION

Father of compassion and God of all comfort, by the power of your Holy Spirit, help _____ "clothe himself/herself with compassion, kindness, humility, gentleness and patience" (2 CORINTHIANS 1:3; COLOSSIANS 3:12).

I pray _____ will bear with others and forgive others as Christ forgave. Over all these virtues help _____ put on love (COLOSSIANS 3:12–14).

PRAY FOR THOSE WHOSE NAME BEGINS WITH **C**.

REFLECTION

> *But there is also a good kind (of pretending), where the pretense leads up to the real thing. When you are not feeling particularly friendly but know you ought to be, the best thing you can do, very often, is to put on a friendly manner and behave as if you were a nicer person than you actually are. And in a few minutes, as we have all noticed, you will be feeling friendlier than you were. Very often the only way to get a quality in reality is to start behaving as if you had it already.[1]*
> —C. S. Lewis, MERE CHRISTIANITY

To "put on airs" derives from the French word *air*, meaning "look or appearance." In essence, it means to masquerade, to pretend you are something you are not. From childhood we play dress-up. As adults we strive to keep up appearances and portray an image through outward adornment. Buying into the belief that "clothes make the man" has created a global three hundred billion-dollar clothing industry. It is astounding how much stock we place on our wardrobe.

The Bible also places great value on how we are to adorn ourselves. It says, "clothe yourselves with compassion, kindness, humility, gentleness and patience."[2] The Greek word for "clothe" is *endyo*, which literally means to "put on." It is an action verb, an imperative.

---

[1] C. S. Lewis, MERE CHRISTIANITY, (New York: Macmillan Publisher, Harper Collins Publishers, 1952) Book IV Chapter 7, 161.

[2] COLOSSIANS 3:12.

Like pulling a shirt over your head or zipping a dress up your back, we are to daily put on Christ.

On days when we are not inclined to get gussied up, Lewis urges, "dress up as Christ."[3] That is, we must ask the Holy Spirit to instill in us Christ-like attributes. Especially when we are not feeling like it, we are to work out our salvation with fear and trembling.[4] The work requires taking an inventory of our inner closet—throwing out old rags and "putting on the new self, which is being renewed in knowledge in the image of our Creator."[5]

This sort of internal closet cleaning is a lifelong process of daily taking stock of our spiritual wardrobe. The initial assessment requires that we acknowledge our sin and trust in the atonement of Christ. Once we do, God will take our filthy rags and "clothe us with garments of salvation and array us in robes of righteousness."[6]

Adorned with salvation! Arrayed in robes of righteousness! What an incredible exchange God is willing to make—our filthy rags for his glorious attire! Have you made the swap?

For further study: 1 TIMOTHY 2:9, 1 PETER 3:3–4

[3] C. S. Lewis, MERE CHRISTIANITY, (New York: Macmillan Publisher, Harper Collins Publishers, 1952) Book IV, Chapter 7, 161.

[4] PHILIPPIANS 2:12–13.

[5] COLOSSIANS 3:10.

[6] ISAIAH 61:10.

CHAPTER 4

DELIGHT IN THE LORD

ADORATION

Praise God for his names, titles, and attributes that begin with **D**.

Praise God, our *deliverer*!

> I love you, O LORD, my strength. The LORD is my rock and my fortress and my deliverer, my God, my rock, in whom I take refuge. He is my shield and the horn of my salvation, my stronghold.
> —PSALM 18:2

Praise God, our *director*!

> This is what the LORD says—your Redeemer, the Holy One of Israel: "I am the LORD your God, who teaches you what is best for you, who directs you in the way you should go."
> —ISAIAH 48:17

Praise God! He is our *dwelling* place!

> LORD, You have been our dwelling place throughout all generations.
> —PSALM 90:1

Praise God! He is the *door*.

> I am the door. If anyone enters by me, he will be saved and will go in and out and find pasture.
> —JOHN 10:9 ESV

Praise God, our *defender*!

> It will be a sign and witness to the LORD Almighty in the land of Egypt. When they cry out to the LORD because of their oppressors, he will send a savior and defender, and he will rescue them.
> —ISAIAH 19:20

> A father to the fatherless, a defender of widows, is God in his holy dwelling.
> —PSALM 68:5

Praise God, the great *designer*!

> For he was looking forward to the city that has foundations, whose designer and builder is God.
> —HEBREWS 11:10 ESV

Praise God for his *divine* nature.

> For since the creation of the world God's invisible qualities—his eternal power and divine nature—have been clearly seen, being understood from what has been made, so that men are without excuse.
> —ROMANS 1:20

PAUSE AND ADORE HIM.

CONFESSION

Father God, I can be so much like Martha, worried and upset, "distracted by many things" (LUKE 10:38–41).

You have said in Your Word, "If you live according to the flesh, you will die, but if by the Spirit you put to death the deeds of the body, you will live" (ROMANS 8:13).

Help me to "Repent therefore, and turn again, that my sins may be blotted out, that times of refreshing may come from the presence of the Lord" (ACTS 3:19–20 ESV).

PAUSE AND CONFESS YOUR SINS.

THANKSGIVING

[*My Help and My Deliverer*] I waited patiently for the LORD; he inclined to me and heard my cry. He drew me up from the pit of destruction, out of the miry bog, and set my feet upon a rock, making my steps secure. He put a new song in my mouth, a song of praise to our God. Many will see and fear and put their trust in the LORD.
—PSALM 40:1–3 ESV

PAUSE AND THANK HIM.

SUPPLICATION

Divine Deliverer, may _____ "not fret because of evil men or be envious of those who do wrong" (PSALM 37:1).

I pray for _____ to "trust in the LORD and do good" (PSALM 37:3).

May _____ "delight in the LORD, that You may give him/her the desires of his/her heart" (PSALM 37:4).

For we know that "the steps of a man are established by the LORD, when he delights in Your way" (PSALM 37:23 ESV).

PRAY FOR THOSE WHOSE NAME BEGINS WITH **D**.

REFLECTION

"Delight yourself in the LORD and he will give you the desires of your heart."[1] Does that mean if you are faithful to God, he promises to give you the grades you want, the job you desire, the car or house you long for, the spouse you yearn for, the healing for which you have prayed? No! The meaning behind this verse and others like it is that when you truly "delight" in the Lord, your desires begin to conform to God's desires and will for your life.

Before transformation of desires can take place, God must "remove from you your heart of stone and give you a heart of flesh."[2] When you confess your sins and trust in Jesus as Lord for your salvation, God fills you with his Spirit. At that moment, he begins the transformation process of "giving you a new heart and putting a new spirit in you."[3]

With this new heart and spirit comes the desire for an abiding relationship with God. As you grow in your knowledge and love of God, you will begin "seeing and savoring him as your dearest friend, Savior, caring protector, provider, and receiving with thanks and worship everything he gives you."[4] Pleasure and delight are found in making his desire ours. "God is most glorified in us when we are most satisfied in Him."[5]

In what are you seeking satisfaction and delight? Is it in things of this world like wealth, status, and material possessions or is it in the things of God? Let us remember the things of this world will fade away[6] but delight found in our eternal triune God promises eternal pleasure.[7]

[1] PSALM 37:4.

[2] EZEKIEL 36:26.

[3] Ibid.

[4] John Piper, "How Do I Delight Myself in the Lord," EPISODE 128 (July 9, 2013), Article in https://www.desiringgod.org.

[5] John Piper, DESIRING GOD: MEDITATIONS OF A CHRISTIAN HEDONIST, (Multnomah, 1986).

[6] 1 JOHN 2:17.

[7] PSALM 16:11.

CHAPTER 5

ENLIGHTENED

ADORATION

Praise God for his names, titles, and attributes that begin with *E*.

Praise our *eternal* God, who established all things, causing all things to endure!

> Call upon the name of the LORD, the Eternal God.
> —GENESIS 21:33

> To him belongs eternal praise.
> —PSALM 111:1, 10

> Your word, O LORD, is eternal; it stands firm in the heavens. Your faithfulness continues through all generations; you established the earth, and it endures. Your laws endure to this day, for all things serve you.
> —PSALM 119:89–91

Praise our *Everlasting* Father!

> LORD, you have been our dwelling place throughout all generations. Before the mountains were born or you brought forth the earth and the world, from everlasting to everlasting you are God.
> —PSALM 90:1–2

> He will be called … Everlasting Father.
> —ISAIAH 9:6

Praise God, our *encourager*!

> The LORD is King for ever and ever; the nations will perish
> from his land. You hear, O LORD, the desires of the afflicted;
> you encourage them, and you listen to their cry, defending
> the fatherless and the oppressed, in order that man, who is of
> the earth, may terrify no more.
> —PSALM 10:16–18

PAUSE AND ADORE HIM.

CONFESSION

> The LORD is in his holy temple; the LORD is on his heavenly
> throne. He observes the sons of men; his eyes examine them.
> The LORD examines the righteous, but the wicked and those who
> love violence his soul hates. On the wicked he will rain fiery
> coals and burning sulfur; a scorching wind will be their lot.
> —PSALM 11:4–6

PAUSE AND CONFESS YOUR SINS.

THANKSGIVING

> But God, being rich in mercy, because of the great love with
> which he loved us, even when we were dead in our trespasses,
> made us alive together with Christ—by grace you have been
> saved—and raised us up with him and seated us with him in the
> heavenly places in Christ Jesus, so that in the coming ages he
> might show the immeasurable riches of his grace in kindness
> toward us in Christ Jesus. For by grace you have been saved
> through faith. And this is not your own doing: it is the gift of
> God, not a result of works, so that no one may boast.
> —EPHESIANS 2:4–9 ESV

PAUSE AND THANK HIM.

SUPPLICATION

Everlasting Father, may I never cease to give thanks for
_____, remembering him/her in my prayers. I ask You
to give _____ the Spirit of wisdom and revelation in the
knowledge of Christ, having the eyes of his/her heart enlightened, that _____ may know what is the hope to which
You have called him/her, what are the riches of Your glorious
inheritance in the saints, and what is the immeasurable greatness
of Your power toward those who believe (EPHESIANS 1:16–19
ESV).

PRAY FOR THOSE WHOSE NAME BEGINS WITH *E*.

REFLECTION

Did you know that spiritually we are all born blind? Familiar with
this condition, the apostle Paul wrote, "The god of this age has
blinded the minds of unbelievers, so that they cannot see the light of
the gospel of the glory of Christ, who is the image of God."[1]

Yet, God revealed himself for all to see,[2] except to those who
refuse to believe. Their minds have been blinded by the "god of this
age," who is Satan. He uses the things of this world like pride, lust,
power, and pleasures to cause spiritual blindness. That is why Paul
prayed, "that the eyes of your heart may be enlightened."[3] Paul petitions the almighty power of God to work in hearts and minds in such
a way that people would gain a greater love and vision of God and
what he has done for us. According to THE NEW BIBLE COMMENTARY,
this prayer is "a prayer for spiritual understanding; the heart here is
a partial synonym for mind, will and spirit, and means the centre of

---

[1] 2 CORINTHIANS 4:4.

[2] ROMANS 1:19.

[3] EPHESIANS 1:18.

perception and decision."[4]

Our need is not necessarily for more knowledge, but for the Spirit of God to give us a vision of his glory. Like the two blind men in MATTHEW 9, we need to "follow Jesus, calling out, 'Have mercy on us, Son of David.'"[5] Let us ask the Lord to open the eyes of our hearts so we can see "the light of life and be satisfied"[6] and sing with the saints, "Be thou my vision, O Lord of my heart!"[7]

---

[4] NEW BIBLE COMMENTARY, (InterVarsity Press, 2010), 1127.

[5] MATTHEW 9:27.

[6] ISAIAH 53:11.

[7] Ancient Irish poem, 6-8th c., attr. St. Dallan Forgaill, translated by Eleanor Hull, 1912.

CHAPTER 6

FRIENDSHIP

ADORATION

Praise God for his names, titles, and attributes that begin with *F*.

Praise God! He is *faithful*.

> Not to us, LORD, not to us, but to your name be the glory, because of your love and faithfulness.
> —PSALM 115:1

> Know therefore that the LORD your God is God; he is the faithful God, keeping his covenant of love to a thousand generations of those who love him and keep his commandments.
> —DEUTERONOMY 7:9

> For the word of the LORD is right and true; he is faithful in all he does.
> —PSALM 33:4

Praise God! He is our *Father.*

> You are my Father, my God, the Rock my Savior.
> —PSALM 89:26

> Abba, Father, everything is possible for you.
> —MARK 14:36

Praise God! He is our *friend.*

> The friendship of the LORD is for those who fear him, and he makes known to them his covenant.
> —PSALM 25:14 ESV

Praise God! He *fights* for you.

> Contend, O LORD, with those who contend with me; fight
> against those who fight against me!
> —PSALM 35:1

> It is the LORD your God who fights for you.
> —DEUTERONOMY 3:22

Praise God! He is a *fire*.

> For the LORD your God is a consuming fire, a jealous God.
> —DEUTERONOMY 4:24

Praise God! He is our *fortress*.

> He is my loving God and my fortress.
> —PSALM 144:2

PAUSE AND ADORE HIM.

CONFESSION

All of us have become like one who is unclean, and all our righteous acts are like filthy rags; we all shrivel up like a leaf, and
like the wind our sins sweep us away. Yet, O LORD, you are our
Father. We are the clay, you are the potter; we are all the work
of your hand.
—ISAIAH 64:6, 8

PAUSE AND CONFESS YOUR SIN.

THANKSGIVING

For God was pleased to have all his fullness dwell in him, and
through him to reconcile to himself all things, whether things on
earth or things in heaven, by making peace through his blood,
shed on the cross.
—COLOSSIANS 1:19

When Jesus saw their faith, he said, "Friend, your sins are forgiven."
—Luke 5:20

Pause and thank him.

Supplication

As Jonathan encouraged and exhorted David, I ask you Lord to give _____ a friend who "helps him/her find strength in God" (1 Samuel 23:16).

May _____ have and be the sort of friend who "warns the idle, encourages the timid, helps the weak, and is patient and kind with everyone" (1 Thessalonians 5:14–15).

I pray _____ will know your word states, "He who walks with the wise grows wise, but a companion of fools suffers harm" (Proverbs 13:20).

Holy Spirit, help _____ choose his/her friends carefully because "the pleasantness of one's friend springs from his earnest counsel" (Proverbs 27:9).

Pray for those whose name begins with F.

Reflection

"If you lay down with dogs, you get up with fleas." This expression warns to watch the company you keep, because without realizing it, habits and traits are picked up. The change is subtle. The next thing you know, you are imitating those around you.

The Bible similarly warns, "He who walks with the wise grows wise, but a companion of fools suffers harm."[1] Paul, writing to the

---
[1] Proverbs 13:20.

Christian church said, "Do not be yoked together with unbelievers. For what do righteousness and wickedness have in common? Or what fellowship can light have with darkness?"[2] In this, Paul warns the believer not to bind themselves with nonbelievers, as it might weaken one's commitments and character. James, the brother of Jesus, wrote to believers as well. "Don't you know friendship with the world is hatred toward God? Anyone who chooses to be a friend of the world becomes an enemy of God."[3]

These verses do not mean disassociation from the world and nonbelievers, but to be mindful of the impact their worldview can have upon your own spiritual and moral life. Even Jesus, our Lord and Master, chose and qualified whom he called friend. He said to those who obeyed his commands, "I no longer call you servants, instead I have called you friends."[4] And he commanded his "friends" to love each other.

God created us to be in loving relationships, with the most important one being our relationship with him, then our relationship with fellow man. Jesus offers himself as our greatest friend. He demonstrated his great love and commitment by "laying down his life for his friends."[5] By his example we learn that true friendship calls for sacrificial love.

With eternal relationships in mind, let us encourage each other in the ways of the Lord and be mindful of doing for others what is best in light of eternity. Let us share the gospel with those we encounter so we can say, "our friends are friends forever" because "the Lord's the Lord of them."[6]

Let us consider how we may spur one another on toward love and good deeds. Let us not give up meeting together, as some are in the habit of doing, but let us encourage one another— and all the more as we see the Day approaching.
—HEBREWS 10:24–25

[2] 2 CORINTHIANS 6:14.

[3] JAMES 4:4.

[4] JOHN 15:12–17.

[5] JOHN 15:13.

[6] Michael W. Smith, "Friends," *The Live Set Album*, (Reunion Records, 1987).

CHAPTER 7

GOOD AND GENEROUS

ADORATION

Praise God for his names, titles, and attributes that begin with *G*.

Praise God! He is *God*.

> Be still, and know that I am God; I will be exalted among the nations, I will be exalted in the earth.
> —PSALM 46:10

> I am God Almighty.
> —GENESIS 35:11

Praise God! He is *great*.

> O Sovereign LORD, you have only begun to show to your servant your greatness and your strong hand. For what god is there in heaven or on earth who can do the deeds and mighty works you do?
> —DEUTERONOMY 3:24

Praise God! He is *good*.

> How great is your goodness!
> —PSALM 31:19

Praise God! He is *glorious*.

> Blessed be your glorious name, which is exalted above all blessing and praise.
> —NEHEMIAH 9:5 ESV

Praise God! He is *gracious*.

> The LORD is gracious and righteous; our God is full of compassion.
> —PSALM 116:5

Praise God! He is the *giver* of every good and perfect gift.

> Every good and perfect gift is from above, coming down from the Father of the heavenly lights, who does not change like shifting shadows.
> —JAMES 1:17

Praise God! He is *gentle*.

> I am gentle and lowly in heart.
> —MATTHEW 11:29

Praise God! He is the *gardener*.

> I am the true vine, and my Father is the gardener.
> —JOHN 15:1

Praise God! He is our *guide*.

> You guide me with your counsel, and afterward you will take me into glory.
> —PSALM 73:24

PAUSE AND ADORE HIM.

CONFESSION

Father God, forgive us all our trespasses, we pray. Every day we sin against you in our thoughts, words, and deeds. We desire to "draw near you with a sincere heart and with full assurance of faith, having our hearts sprinkled to cleanse us from a guilty conscience and having our bodies washed with pure water" (HEBREWS 10:22).

PAUSE AND CONFESS YOUR SINS.

THANKSGIVING

For He has rescued us from the dominion of darkness and brought us into the kingdom of the Son he loves, in whom we have redemption, the forgiveness of sins.
—COLOSSIANS 1:13–14

Now, our God, we give you thanks, and praise your glorious name.
—1 CHRONICLES 29:13

PAUSE AND THANK HIM.

SUPPLICATION

Good and gracious Lord, by the power of your Holy Spirit, "charge _____ not to be haughty, nor to set his/her hopes on the uncertainty of riches, but on God, who richly provides us with everything to enjoy. May _____ do good, be rich in good works, be generous and ready to share, thus storing up treasure for himself/herself as a good foundation for the future, so that _____ may take hold of that which is truly life" (1 TIMOTHY 6:17–19 ESV).

PRAY FOR THOSE WHOSE NAME BEGINS WITH **G**.

REFLECTION

God is great, God is good.
Let us thank Him for our food.
By his hands, we are fed.
Give us Lord our daily bread.

The child's grace above is short and simple, yet profound. This prayer is filled with good doctrine and acknowledges our utter dependence upon God for everything. It teaches some of God's attributes by stating his greatness and goodness, telling of his provision. It reminds us to praise him, thank him, humbly come before him, and ask for our daily needs.

This grace illustrates well that prayers do not have to be eloquent or contain theological jargon to touch the heart of God. As Max Lucado said, "Our prayers may be awkward. Our attempts may be feeble. But since the power of prayer is in the One who hears and not the one who says it, our prayers do make a difference."[1]

Child of God, do you at times doubt whether or not your prayers make a difference? Are you at times hesitant to pray because you do not feel like you have the proper words to say? Our Heavenly Father implores us to "pour out"[2] our heart to him. The Scripture says the Holy Spirit "helps us in our weakness and intercedes for us with groans that words cannot express."[3] In interpreting this passage from ROMANS 8:26–27, Wayne Grudem says,

> It seems more likely that the "sighs" or "groans" here are our groans. When Paul says, "The Spirit helps us in our weakness" (vs. 26), the word translated "helps" (Gk. *sunantilambanomai*)

---

[1] Attributed to Max Lucado.

[2] PSALM 62:8; LAMENTATIONS 2:19.

[3] ROMANS 8:26–27.

is the same word used in LUKE 10:40, where Martha wants Mary to come and *help* her. The word does not indicate that the Holy Spirit prays instead of us, but that the Holy Spirit takes part with us and makes our weak prayers effective. Thus, such sighing or groaning in prayer is best understood to be sighs or groans which we utter, expressing the desires of our heart and spirit, which the Holy Spirit then makes into effective prayer.[4]

Even when you are not able to put into words the expressions of your heart and spirit, pray! "In the last analysis, then, what is prayer but *the language of creaturely dependence* upon that God from whom being itself is derived? ... The intelligent recognition of creature-helplessness leaning upon divine power is the kneeling posture of the soul in prayer."[5]

As God's child, let us humbly express our emotions, desires, and needs to our Creator. God, in his goodness, hears our prayers.[6] Remember, some of the most beautiful petitions are childlike, yet deep and sweet. Let us pray.

---

[4] Wayne Grudem, SYSTEMATIC THEOLOGY, AN INTRODUCTION TO BIBLICAL DOCTRINE, (Zondervan 1994), 382.

[5] B.M. Palmer, THEOLOGY OF PRAYER (Richmond: Presbyterian Committee of Publication, 1894), 15–16.

[6] PSALM 17:1; 55:17; 116:1.

CHAPTER 8

HOLINESS

ADORATION

Praise God for his names, titles, and attributes that begin with *H*.

Praise God! He is *holy*.

> Holy, Holy, Holy is the LORD Almighty; the whole earth is full of his glory.
> —ISAIAH 6:3

> Let them praise your great and awesome name! He is holy! Exalt the LORD our God; worship at his footstool! He is holy! Exalt the LORD our God, and worship at his mountain; for the LORD our God is holy.
> —PSALM 99:3, 5, 9 ESV

> Your ways, O God, are holy. What god is so great as our God? You are the God who performs miracles; you display your power among the peoples. With your mighty arm you redeemed your people.
> —PSALM 77:13–15

Praise the One who is *high* and lofty.

> For this is what the high and lofty One says—He who lives forever, whose name is holy: I live in a high and holy place, but also with him who is contrite and lowly in spirit, to revive the spirit of the lowly and to revive the heart of the contrite.
> —ISAIAH 57:15

Praise the One who is *humble*.

> I am gentle and humble in heart.
> —MATTHEW 11:29

Praise the One who is our *head.*

> For in Christ all the fullness of the Deity lives in bodily form, and you have been given fullness in Christ, who is the head over every power and authority.
> —COLOSSIANS 2:9–10

Praise our great *high priest.*

> Such a high priest meets our need—one who is holy, blameless, pure, set apart from sinners, exalted above the heavens.
> —HEBREWS 7:26

Praise God! He is our *hope.*

> You are God my Savior, and my hope is in you all day long.
> —PSALM 25:5

Praise God! He is our *healer.*

> I am the LORD, who heals you.
> —EXODUS 15:26

Praise God! He is our *helper.*

> The LORD is with me; he is my helper.
> —PSALM 118:7

Praise God! He is our *husband.*

> For your Maker is your husband—the LORD Almighty is his name—the Holy One of Israel is your redeemer; he is called the God of all the earth.
> —ISAIAH 54:4

PAUSE AND ADORE HIM.

CONFESSION

But among you there must not be even a hint of sexual immorality, or of any kind of impurity or of greed, because these are improper for God's holy people. Nor should there be obscenity, foolish talk or course joking, which are out of place, but rather thanksgiving.
—EPHESIANS 5:3–4

For this is the will of God, your sanctification: that you abstain from sexual immorality, that each of you know how to control his own body in holiness and honor, not in the passion of lust…
For God has not called us for impurity, but in holiness.
—1 THESSALONIANS 4:3–5, 7 ESV

PAUSE AND CONFESS YOUR SINS.

THANKSGIVING

I am the LORD, who makes you holy.
—EXODUS 31:13

Unlike the other high priests, he does not need to offer sacrifices day after day, first for his own sins, and then for the sins of the people. He sacrificed for their sins once for all when he offered himself. For the law appoints as high priests men who are weak; but the oath, which came after the law, appointed the Son, who has been made perfect forever.
—HEBREWS 7:27–28

PAUSE AND THANK HIM.

SUPPLICATION

Heavenly Father, it is written in your Holy Word, "Be holy, because I am holy" (1 PETER 1:16).

In view of God's mercy, may _____ "offer his/her body as a living sacrifice, holy and pleasing to God, as a spiritual act of worship" (ROMANS 12:1).

May _____ make "every effort to be found spotless, blameless and at peace with you" (2 PETER 3:14).

By the power of your Holy Spirit, help _____ "live a holy and godly life as he/she looks forward to the day of God" (2 PETER 3:11–12).

PRAY FOR THOSE WHOSE NAME BEGINS WITH *H*.

REFLECTION

Holy, holy, holy!
—ISAIAH 6:3, REVELATION 4:8

In the Bible, holiness is the only attribute of God mentioned three times in succession. God's holiness separates him from all other beings. Holiness is more than perfection, purity, and sinlessness. In essence, it is God's transcendence, that which causes reverential awe.

The Old Testament Hebrew word for holy is *qados*. It means sacred, consecrated, set apart, pure. The New Testament word is *hagios* which has similar meanings. In Jewish liturgy, when something is incredibly important, it is mentioned twice. To mention a word three times places even more emphasis on the matter.

Therefore, "Holy, holy, holy" stresses the weight of the glory of our triune God who calls us to "be holy."

How can one be holy?

As a teenager, my youth pastor urged us to be holy—to live a life set apart. He explained sanctification as a process, the practical steps toward a state of separation, as living unto God and not man. The goal is to become more like Christ. To demonstrate this separation and the effectiveness of Christ in our lives, my pastor encouraged the youth not to drink alcohol. Compliance meant keeping both the laws of man (we were not of legal age to drink) and the laws of God who commands against drunkenness. He made it clear that though Scripture does not prohibit the legal consumption of alcohol, drinking could be a stumbling block. Not that I pretended to be perfect, but because I considered sobriety a tangible way to live a life set apart, I chose not to partake.

CONSIDER 1 PETER 1:15–16. "But just as he who called you is holy, so be holy in all you do; for it is written: 'Be holy, because I am holy.'" Then, ask yourself what practical steps you can take to live as you were called, wholly holy.

Note: The Old Testament and New Testament refer to a "stumbling block" as someone or something that hinders another's relationship with God. Christians should avoid actions that could harm a person's faith in any way. Therefore, a Christian's words and actions should build up rather than trip up another's faith. See LEVITICUS 19:14; EZEKIEL 14:3, 4, 7; MATTHEW 16:23; ROMANS 14:13; 1 CORINTHIANS 1:23.

CHAPTER 9

IMITATOR OF GOD

ADORATION

Praise God for his names, titles, and attributes that begin with *I*.

Praise God! He is the great "*I AM.*"

> God said, "I AM WHO I AM."
> —EXODUS 3:14

> I AM the Bread of Life.
> —JOHN 6:35, 41, 48, 51

> I AM the Light of the World.
> —JOHN 8:12

> I AM the Door of the Sheep.
> —JOHN 10:7, 9

> I AM the Good Shepherd.
> —JOHN 10:11, 14

> I AM the Resurrection and the Life.
> —JOHN 11:25

> I AM the Way, the Truth and the Life.
> —JOHN 14:6

> I AM the True Vine.
> —JOHN 15:1, 5

Praise God! He is our *Immanuel*!

> They shall call his name "Immanuel" (which means *God with us*).
> —MATTHEW 1:23

Praise God! He is our *intercessor.*

> The Spirit himself intercedes for us with groans that words cannot express. And He who searches our hearts knows the mind of the Spirit, because the Spirit intercedes for the saints in accordance with God's will.
> —ROMANS 8:26–27

Praise God, our *instructor.*

> I will instruct you and teach you in the way you should go; I will counsel you and watch over you.
> —PSALM 32:8

Praise God! He is *impartial.*

> You are "a Father who judges each man's work impartially."
> —1 PETER 1:17

Praise our *immortal, invisible* God.

> Now to the King eternal, immortal, invisible, the only God, be honor and glory for ever and ever. Amen.
> —1 TIMOTHY 1:17

PAUSE AND ADORE HIM.

CONFESSION

Father God, your word says, "No immoral, impure or greedy person—such a man is an idolater—has any inheritance in the kingdom of Christ and of God. Let no one deceive you with empty words, for because of such things God's wrath comes on those who are disobedient" (EPHESIANS 5:5–6).

But your iniquities have separated you from your God; your sins have hidden his face from you, so that he will not hear.
—ISAIAH 59:2

Forgive me Lord, I pray!

PAUSE AND CONFESS YOUR SINS.

THANKSGIVING

But you were washed, you were sanctified, you were justified in the name of the Lord Jesus Christ and by the Spirit of our God. —1 CORINTHIANS 6:11b

Thanks be to God that we "were ransomed from the futile ways inherited from our forefathers, not with perishable things such as silver or gold, but with the precious blood of Christ, like that of a lamb without blemish or spot" (1 PETER 1:18–19 ESV).

PAUSE AND THANK HIM.

SUPPLICATION

Immortal, invisible God, we thank you for giving Jesus Christ as the "radiance of Your glory, the exact representation of Your being" (HEBREWS 1:3).

By the power of your Holy Spirit, give _____ the desire to "be an imitator of God. Help _____ live a life of love, just as Christ loved us and gave himself up for us as a fragrant offering and sacrifice to God" (EPHESIANS 5:1).

PRAY FOR THOSE WHOSE NAME BEGINS WITH I.

Reflection

In Exodus 3:14, God said, "I AM WHO I AM." The statement 'I AM" is a form of the Hebrew name of God YHWH or Yahweh and is related to the verb "to be." It is a title God gave himself in Exodus. In this all-inclusive expression, the Godhead is stating he is the sovereign, self-existent, self-sufficient, unchanging, ever-present, eternal God incarnate.

In the book of John, Jesus made seven "I AM" declarations about himself. In Mark 8:29, he asked, "Who do the people say I am?" After listening to their response, his question took a personal turn. "What about you? Who do you say that I am?"

My friend, who do you say God is? Is God the Lord of your life or are you trying to run and rule your life autonomously, thinking you have it all under control? Guard yourself against "I am" statements like the one in William Ernest Henley's poem *Invictus*, "I am the master of my fate, I am the captain of my soul." Humbly come before God's throne of grace and acknowledge your utter dependence upon the one and only, omniscient, omnipresent, omnipotent God, and surrender total control of your life to the great "I AM."

CHAPTER 10

JUST

ADORATION

Praise God for his names, titles, and attributes that begin with *J*.

Praise God! He is *just*.

> I will praise you, O LORD, with all my heart; I will tell of all your wonders. I will be glad and rejoice in you; I will sing to your name, O Most High. The LORD is known by his justice.
> —PSALM 9:1–2, 16

> For the LORD is righteous, he loves justice; upright men will see his face.
> —PSALM 11:7

> For the word of the LORD is right and true; He is faithful in all he does. The Lord loves righteousness and justice; the earth is full of his unfailing love.
> —PSALM 33:4–5

> The works of his hands are faithful and just; all his precepts are trustworthy.
> —PSALM 111:7

Praise God! He is the *justifier.*

> It is to show his righteousness at the present time, so that he might be just and the justifier of the one who has faith in Jesus.
> —ROMANS 3:26 ESV

Praise God! He is our righteous *judge.*

> God is a righteous judge, and a God who feels indignation every day.
> —PSALM 7:11

Praise God! He is *jealous* for his own.

> Do not worship any other god, for the LORD, whose name is Jealous, is a jealous God.
> —EXODUS 34:14

> I, the LORD your God, am a jealous God.
> —EXODUS 20:5

Praise God! He is *Jesus.*

> You are to give him the name Jesus, because he will save his people from their sins.
> —MATTHEW 1:21

Praise God! In him is *joy.*

> The joy of the LORD is your strength.
> —NEHEMIAH 8:10

> You have made known to me the path of life; you will fill me with joy in your presence, with eternal pleasures at your right hand.
> —PSALM 16:11

PAUSE AND ADORE HIM.

CONFESSION

> For we ourselves were once foolish, disobedient, led astray, slaves to various passions and pleasures, passing our days in malice and envy, hated by others and hating others.
> —TITUS 3:3 ESV

> God will bring to judgment both the righteous and the wicked.
> —ECCLESIASTES 3:17

PAUSE AND CONFESS YOUR SINS.

THANKSGIVING

But when the kindness and love of God our Savior appeared, he saved us, not because of righteous things we had done, but because of his mercy. He saved us through the washing of rebirth and renewal by the Holy Spirit, whom he poured out on us generously through Jesus Christ our Savior, so that, having been justified by his grace, we might become heirs having the hope of eternal life.
—TITUS 3:4–7

PAUSE AND THANK HIM.

SUPPLICATION

Jesus, You are the One who has shown us what is good and what is required of us. By the power of your Holy Spirit, show _____ how to "act justly, and to love mercy and to walk humbly with our God" (MICAH 6:8).

PRAY FOR THOSE WHOSE NAME BEGINS WITH *J*.

REFLECTION

But now a righteousness from God, apart from the law has been made known, to which the Law and the Prophets testify. This righteousness from God comes through faith in Jesus Christ to all who believe. There is no difference, for all have sinned and fall short of the glory of God, and are justified freely by his grace through the redemption that came by Christ Jesus. God presented him as a sacrifice of atonement, through faith in his blood. He did this to demonstrate his justice; because in forbearance he had

left the sins committed beforehand unpunished—he did it to demonstrate his justice at the present time, so as to be just and the one who justifies those who have faith in Jesus.
—ROMANS 3:22–26

How can a holy and righteous God remain just when he forgives peoples' sins? In doing so, does he violate his attribute of justice, which requires a penalty to be paid for sins? The answer is found in the inerrant, infallible word of God.

The Bible teaches that God is holy, which means sinless, set apart. The word "sin" originated from an archery term meaning to "miss the mark." All men have sinned, or missed the mark, of God's holy standard.

Scripture also teaches that God is just. He requires a penalty to be paid for the violation of his righteous standard. In order to maintain his justice, he could not let the sins of man go unpunished. A penalty had to be paid.

In Old Testament times, a priest ceremonially and symbolically made propitiation—the satisfaction of divine justice—with the blood of goats and lambs. These sacrifices served as an adumbration, a dim glimmering of what was to come (Christ). The sacrifices did not satisfy the righteous standard of God. "It is impossible for the blood of bulls and goats to take away sin."[1] Therefore, a holy, righteous, and pure sacrifice had to be made. Hence, God sent his son, Jesus Christ, as atonement for our sins. By doing this, God became just and the justifier of our faith.

As you contemplate the atonement, consider reading THE CROSS OF CHRIST by John Stott.[2] With your reading, listen to the following sermon and a song. The sermon I recommend is "The Vindication of God,"[3] preached by Dr. D. Martyn Lloyd-Jones, considered to be one of the finest expository preachers of the twentieth century. In

[1] HEBREWS 10:4.

[2] John Stott, THE CROSS OF CHRIST, (IVP Books, 2006).

[3] Dr. D. Martyn Lloyd-Jones, VINDICATION OF GOD, Banner of Truth, 1990.
SERMON LINK: HTTPS://WWW.MLJTRUST.ORG/SERMONS-ONLINE/ROMANS-3-25-26/
THE-VINDICATION-OF-GOD/

this exposition of ROMANS 3:25–26, Lloyd-Jones explains the atonement and how Christ's death accomplished our justification. It can be found online at MLJTrust.org.

The song, "Come Behold the Wondrous Mystery,"[4] proclaims doctrinal truth—the eternal existence of God, his incarnation, redemption, his deity, Christ's federal headship, his holiness, his vicarious atonement, God's justice, God's decree, God's effectual call, Christ's resurrection, and the hope of glory and our resurrected bodies. Wow!

May a deeper knowledge and understanding of these theological truths cause us to be effusive in our praise and thanksgiving to God who is just and the justifier of our faith.

---

[4] Matt Papa, "Come Behold the Wondrous Mystery," *Look & Live Album*, (The Summit Church Publishing, 2013).

CHAPTER 11

KNOWLEDGEABLE

ADORATION

Praise God for his names, titles, and attributes that begin with **K.**

Praise God! He is *King of kings*!

> All praise be to God, "the blessed and only Sovereign, the King of kings and Lord of lords, who alone has immortality, who dwells in unapproachable light, whom no one has ever seen or can see. To him be honor and eternal dominion. Amen."
> —1 TIMOTHY 6:15 ESV

> On his robe and on his thigh he has a name written: KING OF KINGS AND LORD OF LORDS.
> —REVELATION 19:16

Praise be to the *King forever*!

> The LORD is King forever and ever.
> —PSALM 10:16

Praise be to the *King of glory*!

> Who is he, this King of glory? The LORD Almighty—he is the King of glory!
> —PSALM 24:10

Praise God! He is our *keeper.*

> The LORD is your keeper; the LORD is your shade at your right hand.
> —PSALM 121:5

Praise God! He is *kind.*

> The LORD is faithful in all his words and kind in all his works.
> —PSALM 145:13

Praise God! He is the One who *knows all things.*

> The Mighty One, God, the LORD! The Mighty One, God,
> The LORD! He knows.
> —JOSHUA 22:22

> He knows everything.
> —1 JOHN 3:20

PAUSE AND ADORE HIM.

CONFESSION

> Do you presume on the riches of his kindness and forbearance
> and patience, not knowing that God's kindness is meant to lead
> you to repentance? But because of your hard and impenitent
> heart you are storing up wrath for yourself on the day of wrath
> when God's righteous judgment will be revealed.
> —ROMANS 2:4–5 ESV

> The heart knows its own bitterness.
> —PROVERBS 14:10

Lord, I repent of my sins. Please "hear in heaven and forgive the
sin of your servants, your people, and teach us the good way in
which we should walk" (1 KINGS 8:36 ESV).

PAUSE AND CONFESS YOUR SINS.

THANKSGIVING

Thanks be to God! "He delivered us from darkness and transferred us to the kingdom of his beloved Son, in whom we have redemption, the forgiveness of sins" (COLOSSIANS 1:13 ESV).

PAUSE AND THANK HIM.

SUPPLICATION

The LORD gives wisdom; from his mouth come knowledge and understanding.
—PROVERBS 2:6

All-knowing King of kings, I pray, "The Spirit of the LORD will rest on _____, the Spirit of wisdom and of understanding, the Spirit of counsel and of power, the Spirit of knowledge and of the fear of the LORD – and that _____ will delight in the fear of the LORD" (ISAIAH 11:2–3).

I humbly ask, "for wisdom to enter _____'s heart and knowledge to be pleasant to _____'s soul" (PROVERBS 2:10).

Please "fill _____ with the knowledge of Your will through all spiritual wisdom and understanding. I pray this in order that _____ may live a life worthy of the Lord and may please You in every way" (COLOSSIANS 1:9–12).

PRAY FOR THOSE WHOSE NAME BEGINS WITH *K*.

REFLECTION

Wisdom is the right use of knowledge. To know is not to be wise. Many men know a great deal, and are all the greater fools for it. There is no fool so great a fool as a knowing fool. But to know how to use knowledge is to have wisdom.
—Charles Haddon Spurgeon, *Spurgeon's Sermon Volume* 17:1817

Once, after hearing my brother-in-law regurgitate a bunch of sports statistics, my uncle replied, "Boy, you know you have a head full of useless information." My brother-in-law took his comment in stride and agreed, though these facts were of interest, they had no application to his day-to-day life.

The same can be said of many of us. We possess a head full of biblical knowledge and can recite scriptural truths, but we do not apply them to our lives. Jesus warned, "Woe to you! You appear to people as righteous but on the inside you are full of hypocrisy and wickedness."[1] Our head knowledge of God proves worthless to life and godliness unless applied prudently through faith and trust resulting in obedience and love.

Wisdom and knowledge are found in God's Word and gained through a relationship with Jesus Christ.[2] Proverbs states, "For the LORD gives wisdom, and from his mouth come knowledge and understanding."[3] They come as gifts from God, as well as a result of seeking, searching, and asking. "If any of you lacks wisdom," James says, "he should ask God, who gives generously to all."[4] He then writes, "Who is wise and understanding among you? Let him

---

[1] MATTHEW 23:27–28.

[2] 1 CORINTHIANS 1:30; COLOSSIANS 2:3.

[3] PROVERBS 2:6.

[4] JAMES 1:5.

show it by his good life, by deeds done in humility that comes from wisdom."[5]

As stated earlier, knowledge for knowledge's sake is worthless. In order to be beneficial, it must be applied prudently. Practically, wisdom is shown when we apply our Bible readings and our preacher's teachings and become obedient doers of God's Word. Therefore, "Be very careful, then, how you live—not as unwise, but as wise, making the most of every opportunity."[6] "Whatever you have learned or received or heard or seen" in faithful followers of Christ, "put it into practice."[7]

---

[5] JAMES 3:13.

[6] EPHESIANS 5:15.

[7] PHILIPPIANS 4:9.

CHAPTER 12

LET LIGHT SHINE

ADORATION

Praise God for his names, titles, and attributes that begin with *L*.

Praise the *Lord of lords*!

> For the LORD your God is God of gods and Lord of lords, the great God, mighty and awesome, who shows no partiality and accepts no bribes.
> —DEUTERONOMY 10:17

Praise God! He is *love*.

> How precious is your steadfast love, O God! The children of mankind take refuge in the shadow of your wings.
> —PSALM 36:7 ESV

Praise God! He is the giver of *life*!

> Jesus said, "I am the bread of life"; "I am the living bread that came down from heaven."
> —JOHN 6:35, 48, 51

Praise God! He is *light*.

> I am the light of the world. Whoever follows me will never walk in darkness, but will have the light of life.
> —JOHN 8:12

Praise God! He is our *lamp*.

> For it is you who light my lamp; the LORD my God lightens my darkness.
> —PSALM 18:28 ESV

Praise the *Lamb of God!*

Behold, the Lamb of God, who takes away the sin of the world.
—JOHN 1:29 ESV

PAUSE AND ADORE HIM.

CONFESSION

God of all light, you "reveal the deep things of darkness and bring utter darkness into light" (JOB 12:22).

Expose those things in my heart and mind that bring grief and cause shame to your holy name, in order that I may acknowledge my sins and receive forgiveness in your name.

PAUSE AND CONFESS YOUR SINS.

THANKSGIVING

But if we walk in the light, as he is in the light, we have fellowship with one another, and the blood of Jesus, his Son, purifies us from all sin.
—1 JOHN 1:7

I have come into the world as a light, so that no one who believes in me should stay in darkness.
—JOHN 12:46

Thank you that "You, LORD, are my lamp; You turn my darkness into light" (2 SAMUEL 22:29).

PAUSE AND THANK HIM.

SUPPLICATION

Light of the world, "let the light of your face shine upon _____ " so the light of Christ may shine through _____ (PSALM 4:6).

Fill _____ with your Holy Spirit so that he/she will "do all things without grumbling or disputing, that _____ may be blameless and innocent, a child of God without blemish in the midst of a crooked and twisted generation, among whom _____ shines as a light in the world, holding fast to the word of life, so that in the day of Christ _____ may be proud that he/she did not run in vain or labor in vain" (PHILIPPIANS 2:14–16 ESV).

Let _____ 's "light shine before men, that they may see his/her good deeds and glorify our Father in heaven" (MATTHEW 5:16).

PRAY FOR THOSE WHOSE NAME BEGINS WITH **L**.

REFLECTION

General revelation and special revelation are two ways God has chosen to reveal himself to mankind. General revelation refers to the universal truths that can be known about God through nature.[1] Special revelation refers to the more specific truths that can be known about God through the Bible and the supernatural workings of the Holy Spirit.

In today's reading about the Magi, note how God used general and special revelation. He used Old Testament prophecy, nature's star, and the supernatural means to reveal that the "light of the

---

[1] PSALM 19:1–2; ROMANS 1:19–20.

world"[2] had come. Today, he uses those same means, as well as followers of Jesus Christ, to shine his light.

In the New Testament we read Jesus, the Bright and Morning Star,[3] came to earth in all brilliance as "the light of the world,"[4] as "the true light that gives light to every man."[5] His coming was predicted in NUMBERS, "A star will come out of Jacob; a scepter will rise out of Israel."[6] Knowledge of this prophecy, given more than fourteen hundred years before it came to be, caused the Magi to follow the star in the east.[7] The light irresistibly drew these men and guided them to Jesus.[8]

Ponder this thought: The "Father of heavenly lights"[9] draws men to himself and calls them to be "the light of the world."[10] Through Paul, he bids his followers to "live as children of light" and states "the fruit of light consists in all goodness, righteousness and truth." He urges us to "find out what pleases the Lord. Have nothing to do with the fruitless deeds of darkness, but rather expose them."[11]

Gaze into the vast night sky. Look at the infinite galaxies. Think about how the great Creator God of the universe has "determined the number of stars and calls each by name."[12] Think about how one star, light-years away, dispels the darkness around it. Its light reaches earth with twinkling brilliance.

The same God who knows each star by name, created you, redeemed you, and summoned you by name[13] and said, "You are

---

[2] JOHN 8:12.

[3] REVELATION 22:16.

[4] JOHN 8:12.

[5] JOHN 1:9.

[6] NUMBERS 24:17.

[7] MATTHEW 2.

[8] MATTHEW 2:9.

[9] JAMES 1:17.

[10] MATTHEW 5:14.

[11] EPHESIANS 5:8–11.

[12] PSALM 147:4.

[13] ISAIAH 43:1.

the light of the world."[14] God desires his followers to be beacons of light who dispel darkness and "shine like stars in the universe as they hold out the word of life."[15]

Examine your life. Are you radiating Christ's light through your words, attitudes, and actions in such a way that others are drawn and directed to the Light of Life? Pray for the Holy Spirit to infuse you. Let your "light shine before men, that they may see your good deeds and praise your Father in heaven."[16]

[14] MATTHEW 5:14.

[15] PHILIPPIANS 2:15.

[16] MATTHEW 5:16.

CHAPTER 13

MERCIFUL

ADORATION

Praise God for his names, titles, and attributes that begin with *M*.

Praise God! He is our *Maker*.

> Oh come, let us worship and bow down; let us kneel before the LORD our Maker! For he is our God, and we are the people of his pasture, the sheep of his hand.
> —PSALM 95:6

Praise God! He is *majestic*.

> Who among the gods is like you, O LORD? Who is like you, majestic in holiness, awesome in glory, working wonders?
> —EXODUS 15:11

> The LORD reigns; he is robed in majesty.
> —PSALM 93:1

Praise his *Majestic Glory*!

> He (Christ) received honor and glory from God the Father when the voice came to him from the Majestic Glory saying, "This is my beloved Son, with him I am well pleased."
> —2 PETER 1:17

Praise God! He is *mighty*.

> Mightier than the thunder of the great waters, mightier than the breakers of the sea, the LORD on high is mighty!
> —PSALM 93:4

Praise God! He is our *Master*.

> You have a Master in heaven.
> —COLOSSIANS 4:1

Praise God! He is our *mediator*.

> There is one God, and there is one mediator between God
> and men, the man Christ Jesus.
> —1 TIMOTHY 2:5

Praise God! He is the *Morning Star*.

> I (Jesus) am the Root and the Offspring of David, and the
> bright Morning Star.
> —REVELATION 22:16

Praise God! He is *merciful*.

> My soul glorifies the Lord and my spirit rejoices in God
> my Savior, for he has been mindful of the humble state of
> his servant. His mercy extends to those who fear him, from
> generation to generation.
> —LUKE 1:46–48; 50

> You are a gracious and merciful God.
> —NEHEMIAH 9:31

> Praise be to the LORD, for he has heard my cry for mercy.
> The LORD is my strength and my shield; my heart trusts in
> him, and I am helped. My heart leaps for joy and I will give
> thanks to him in song.
> —PSALM 28:6–7

PAUSE AND ADORE HIM.

Confession

God, have mercy on me, a sinner.
—Luke 18:13

Remember, O Lord, your great mercy and love, for they are
from old. Remember not the sins of my youth and my rebellious
ways; according to your love remember me, for you are good,
O Lord.
—Psalm 25:6–7

Pause and confess your sins.

Thanksgiving

Who is a God like you, who pardons sin and forgives the trans-
gression of the remnant of his inheritance? You do not stay
angry forever but delight to show mercy. You will again have
compassion on us; you will tread our sins underfoot and hurl all
our iniquities into the depths of the sea.
—Micah 7:18–19

Praise be to the God and Father of our Lord Jesus Christ! In his
great mercy he has given us new birth into a living hope through
the resurrection of Jesus Christ from the dead.
—1 Peter 1:3

Pause and thank him.

Supplication

Most High, you are kind to the ungrateful and wicked.
—Luke 6:35

May _____ "be merciful, just as our Father is merciful"
(Luke 6:36).

By the power of your Holy Spirit, help _____ to graciously "forgive as the Lord forgave him/her" (COLOSSIANS 3:13).

May _____ know that "judgment without mercy will be shown to anyone who has not been merciful" (JAMES 2:13).

PRAY FOR THOSE WHOSE NAME BEGINS WITH *M*.

REFLECTION

Blessed be the God and Father of our Lord Jesus Christ, the Father of mercies and God of all comfort, who comforts us in all our afflictions, so that we may be able to comfort those who are in affliction, with the comfort with which we ourselves are comforted by God.
—1 CORINTHIANS 1:3–4 ESV

"You don't know how merciful a man is until you are put at his mercy." My father-in-law, George Campsen, Jr., made this statement often as he related it to his experience at his beloved alma mater, The Citadel.

The Citadel, the Military College of South Carolina, is a school that provides students with a classical military style education. Leadership, discipline, and character development are essential parts of the educational experience. "But the real education", George said, "was the education in human nature" gained through the Fourth Class System. Under this system, freshmen, or "knobs" as they are called, come under the authority of upperclassmen. The upperclassmen prepare knobs for leadership through rigorous and stressful demands where knobs learn the habits of fitness, self-discipline, study, teamwork and accountability. Knobs are largely at the mercy of upperclassmen.

My father-in-law was first of three generations of Campsens to attend the Citadel. He, with my husband and our sons, witnessed a startling principle in play. The knobs that complained the most about abusive upperclassmen often became the most tyrannical upperclassmen. This experience gave them a first-hand education in human nature. Human nature, in stark contrast to God's holy and merciful nature, was on display as these men in my family witnessed some knobs who cried out for mercy later became merciless.

"God's mercy means God's goodness toward those in misery and distress."[1] God's mercy encompasses his kindness, favor, and grace, and is shown in his heartfelt compassion for his beloved.

Beloved, how do you respond to mercy pleas? Are you kind and gracious? Do you show compassion toward those in distress? Have you shown forbearance toward your offenders? Are you merciful toward those subject to your authority? When considering how you are going to treat another, remember Jesus' teaching, "Blessed are the merciful, for they will be shown mercy."[2]

---

[1] Wayne Grudem, SYSTEMATIC THEOLOGY: AN INTRODUCTION TO BIBLICAL DOCTRINE, (Zondervan 1994), 200.

[2] MATTHEW 5:7.

CHAPTER 14

No One Take You Captive

Adoration

Praise God for his names, titles, and attributes that begin with *N*.

Praise God! Yours is the *name above all names.*

> God exalted him to the highest place and gave him the name that is above every name, that at the name of Jesus every knee should bow, in heaven and on earth and under the earth, and every tongue confess that Jesus Christ is Lord, to the glory of God the Father.
> —Philippians 2:9–11

> Let them praise the name of the Lord, for his name alone is exalted; his splendor is above the earth and the heavens.
> —Psalm 148:13

> Blessed be your glorious name, and may it be exalted above all blessing and praise.
> —Nehemiah 9:5

Praise God! There is *none* like You.

> O Sovereign Lord! There is no one like you, and there is no God but you.
> —2 Samuel 7:22

> There is none holy like the Lord; for there is none besides you; there is no Rock like our God.
> —1 Samuel 2:2

> There is none like you, O Lord; you are great, and your name is great in might.
> —Jeremiah 10:6 ESV

Praise God! He is the *nourisher* of our souls.

> Christ, you are "the Head, from whom the whole body, nourished and knit together through its joints and ligaments, grows with a growth that is from God" (COLOSSIANS 2:19 ESV).

Praise God! He is the *good news*!

> How beautiful on the mountains are the feet of the messenger who brings good news, the good news of peace and salvation, the news that the God of Israel reigns!
> —ISAIAH 52:7 NLT

PAUSE AND ADORE HIM.

CONFESSION

See, the Lord is coming with thousands upon thousands of his holy ones to judge everyone, and to convict all the ungodly of all the ungodly acts they have done in the ungodly way, and of all the harsh words ungodly sinners have spoken. These men are grumblers and faultfinders; they follow their own evil desires; they boast about themselves and flatter others for their own advantage.
—JUDE 14–16

PAUSE AND CONFESS YOUR SINS.

THANKSGIVING

Everyone who believes in him receives forgiveness of sins through his name.
—ACTS 10:43

Therefore, "I will bow down toward your holy temple and will praise your name for your love and your faithfulness, for you have exalted above all things your name and your word."
—PSALM 138:2

PAUSE AND THANK HIM.

SUPPLICATION

Spirit of Truth, "see to it that no one takes _____ captive through hollow and deceptive philosophy, which depends on human tradition and the basic principles of this world rather than on Christ" (COLOSSIANS 2:8).

May _____ "no longer be like an infant, tossed back and forth by the waves, and blown here and there by every wind of teaching and by the cunning and craftiness of men in their deceitful scheming" (EPHESIANS 4:14).

Holy Spirit, guard _____'s heart and mind so that he/she is not "enticed to turn away and worship other gods and bow down to them" (DEUTERONOMY 11:16).

Please "keep _____ as the apple of your eye; hide _____ in the shadow of your wings" (PSALM 17:8).

PRAY FOR THOSE WHOSE NAME BEGINS WITH *N*.

REFLECTION

My maternal grandmother, Nell Lightsey, quipped, "What is the old maid's favorite Bible verse?" The answer? "If any man would come after me, let him." This witticism illustrates the danger of taking a Bible verse out of context, letting it say what you want it to say, rather than what it truly says. In doing so, the truths of Scripture get twisted.

The Bible warns, "the time will come when men will not put up with sound doctrine. Instead, to suit their own desires, they will gather around them a great number of teachers to say what their itching ears want to hear."[1]

Not unlike Paul's admonition in COLOSSIANS 2:8, Peter warns believers everywhere, "be on your guard so that you may not be carried away by error but grow in the grace and knowledge of our Lord and Savior Jesus Christ."[2] In order not to be misled, spend time in the Word and ask the Holy Spirit to guide you as you read and pray. Like the Bereans in ACTS 17, "examine the Scriptures every day to see if what you are being taught is true."[3]

When I question if what is being taught is true, I open the Bible. I read the entire passage and try to discern what is being said. I look up other passages on the subject and apply the principle—*let Scripture interpret Scripture.* I ask the Holy Spirit to give me wisdom and insight. I consult those more mature in the faith and read Bible commentaries, dictionaries, and concordances. This practice has proved helpful in discerning biblical fact from fallacy.

Diligent study and consistent reading of the inerrant, infallible word of God will keep you from being carried away by error and enable you to discern fact from fallacy. As Paul charged Timothy,

---

[1] 2 TIMOTHY 4:3.

[2] 2 PETER 3:17.

[3] ACTS 17:11.

I exhort you, "Do your best to present yourselves to God as one approved, a workman who does not need to be ashamed and who correctly handles the word of truth."[4]

Several of my favorite Bible study resources:

THE STRONGEST NIV EXHAUSTIVE CONCORDANCE (Zondervan 1999, 1990).

THE NEW BIBLE COMMENTARY, 21ST CENTURY EDITION (InterVarsity Press, 2010).

NEW BIBLE DICTIONARY, THIRD EDITION (InterVarsity Press, 1962).

WAYNE GRUDEM, SYSTEMATIC THEOLOGY, AN INTRODUCTION TO BIBLICAL DOCTRINE (Zondervan, 1994).

---

[4] 2 TIMOTHY 2:15.

CHAPTER 15

OBEDIENT

ADORATION

Praise God for His names, titles, and attributes that begin with *O*.

Praise God! He is the *one and only*.

> The Word became flesh and made his dwelling among us. We have seen his glory, the glory of the one and only Son, who came from the Father, full of grace and truth.
> —JOHN 1:14

Praise God! He is the Alpha and *Omega*.

> "I am the Alpha and the Omega," says the Lord God, "who is and who was and who is to come, the Almighty."
> —REVELATION 1:8

Praise God! He is *omniscient*.

> Who has measured the Spirit of the LORD, or what man shows him his counsel? Whom did he consult, and who made him understand? Who taught him the path of justice, and taught him knowledge, and showed him the way of understanding?
> —ISAIAH 40:13–14 ESV

Praise God! He is *omnipresent*.

> Where shall I go from your Spirit? Or where shall I flee from your presence? If I ascend to heaven, you are there! If I make my bed in Sheol, you are there! If I take the wings of the morning and dwell in the uttermost parts of the sea, even there your hand shall lead me and your right hand shall hold me.
> —PSALM 139:7–10 ESV

Praise God! He is *omnipotent*.

> God thunders wondrously with his voice; he does great
> things that we cannot comprehend.
> —JOB 37:5 ESV

> Thus says the LORD, your Redeemer, who formed you from
> the womb: "I am the Lord, who made all things, who alone
> stretched out the heavens, who spread out the earth by
> myself."
> —ISAIAH 44:24 ESV

PAUSE AND ADORE HIM.

CONFESSION

> "Only acknowledge your guilt, that you rebelled against the
> LORD your God and scattered your favors among foreigners
> under every green tree, and that you have not obeyed my voice,"
> declares the LORD.
> —JEREMIAH 3:13 ESV

PAUSE AND CONFESS YOUR SINS.

THANKSGIVING

> For God so loved the world that he gave his one and only Son,
> that whoever believes in him shall not perish but have eternal
> life.
> —JOHN 3:16

PAUSE AND THANK HIM.

SUPPLICATION

Omniscient, omnipotent, and omnipresent Lord, I pray that
_____ may "be careful to obey God's law; not turning
from it to the right or left. May _____ strive not to let the
Book of the Law depart from his/her mouth; meditate on it day
and night, so that he/she may be careful to do everything written in it. Then _____ will be prosperous and successful"
(JOSHUA 1:7–8).

PRAY FOR THOSE WHOSE NAME BEGINS WITH *O*.

REFLECTION

> *You have made known to me the path of life; you will fill
> me with joy in your presence, with eternal pleasures at
> your right hand.*
> —PSALM 16:11

When I read the Christian acronym for OBEY, *Order By Everyday
Yielding*, I immediately thought of a story my sister-in-law told about
my niece. As a young, strong-willed child, my niece did not want to
yield to her mother's instruction. When directed, she responded, "I
don't want to obey you, I want to obey me!"

Often, we possess that same unyielding spirit in response to what
God has commanded. We do not want to follow his rules. We think
rule following will squelch our enjoyment. We want to do things our
own way. We think we know what will bring the most satisfaction. We
want to follow our own desire rather than God's. We think "obeying
me" will bring the most pleasure. Yet, often doing things our own
way, in disobedience to God and his Word, brings pain.

Is obedience to God's Word a struggle of yours? Pray for the Holy
Spirit to help you obey God's commands. The next time you think

yielding to God is a surefire way to kill joy, remember disobedience may seem pleasurable for a season; however, it will reap a painful harvest. Like parental instruction to a child, God's directives are intended for our ultimate good. "Be careful to obey all these regulations I am giving you," Scripture says, "so that it may go well with you and your children after you, because you will be doing what is good and right in the eyes of the LORD your God" (DEUTERONOMY 12:28).

CHAPTER 16

PERSEVERANCE

ADORATION

Praise God for his names, titles, and attributes that begin with *P*.

Praise God! He is *perfect* and *pure*.

> The law of the LORD is perfect, reviving the soul; the testimony of the LORD is sure, making wise the simple; the precepts of the LORD are right, rejoicing the heart; the commandment of the LORD is pure, enlightening the eyes.
> —PSALM 19:7–8 ESV

> As for God, his way is perfect; the word of the LORD is flawless.
> —PSALM 18:30

Praise God! He is the *perfecter*.

> Let us fix our eyes on Jesus, the author and perfecter of our faith.
> —HEBREWS 12:2

Praise God! He is *powerful*.

> Say to God, "How awesome are your deeds! So great is your power that your enemies cringe before you."
> —PSALM 66:3

> The voice of the LORD is powerful; the voice of the LORD is majestic.
> —PSALM 29:4

Praise God! He is our *potter*.

> Yet, O LORD, you are our Father. We are the clay, you are the potter; we are all the work of your hand.
> —ISAIAH 64:8

Praise God! He is *patient*.

> The Lord is not slow in keeping his promise, as some understand slowness. Instead he is patient with you, not wanting anyone to perish, but everyone to come to repentance.
> —2 PETER 3:9

> Bear in mind that our Lord's patience means salvation.
> —2 PETER 3:15

Praise God! He is our *powerful prophet*.

> "About Jesus of Nazareth," they replied. "He was a prophet, powerful in word and deed before God and all the people."
> —LUKE 24:19

Praise God! He is our *priest*.

> You are a priest forever.
> —PSALM 110:4

Praise God! He is our *Prince of Peace*.

> And he will be called Wonderful Counselor, Mighty God, Everlasting Father, Prince of Peace.
> —ISAIAH 9:6

PAUSE AND ADORE HIM.

CONFESSION

If a man does not repent, God will whet his sword; he has bent and readied his bow; he has prepared for him his deadly weapons, making his arrows fiery shafts.
—PSALM 7:12–13 ESV

PAUSE AND CONFESS YOUR SINS.

THANKSGIVING

Here is a trustworthy saying that deserves full acceptance: Christ Jesus came into the world to save sinners—of whom I am the worst. But for that very reason I was shown mercy so that in me, the worst of sinners, Christ Jesus might display his unlimited patience as an example to those who would believe on him and receive eternal life.
—1 TIMOTHY 1:15–16

PAUSE AND THANK HIM.

SUPPLICATION

Perfect and powerful Lord, may _____ "consider it pure joy whenever he/she faces trials of many kinds." May _____ "know that the testing of his/her faith develops perseverance" (JAMES 1:2–3).

"Perseverance must finish its work so that _____ may be mature and complete, not lacking anything" (JAMES 1:4).

May _____ "Look to the LORD and his strength; seek his face always" (PSALM 105:4).

PRAY FOR THOSE WHOSE NAME BEGINS WITH *P*.

REFLECTION

The apostle Paul describes the Christian life as a foot race, with the believer running toward a heavenly reward.[1] This race has been described as a marathon rather than a sprint, which takes perseverance just to finish.

In order to finish life's race well, HEBREWS 10, calls believers to persevere. It is followed by Chapter 11's exaltation of Old Testament saints who endured by faith, though they did not receive the promise (Christ) we have received. Yet, these saints kept a heavenly focus and were commended for their faith.

Like a marathon, the Christian life of faith can be grueling. The race marked out may be long and hard, and include peaks and valleys, along with twists and turns. In order to run the race, we must be in shape. The Bible tells us to "throw off everything that hinders and the sin that so easily entangles and run with perseverance the race marked out for us… Let us fix our eyes on Jesus."[2]

I remember my first race at a high school track meet. Drafted at the last minute to run the 200-meter sprint, I had not been coached. Placed on the outside of the track, I had no idea the rules for that race required the runners stay in their lane. As you have probably guessed, a few steps out of the block, I cut toward the inside of the track. The tactic worked to my advantage, but it cost me the race. I was disqualified because I had not competed according to the rules. There had been no preparation, no training, no guidance, no direction, and no prize.

Thankfully, the Christian life of faith is not like my first race. We have been given the rulebook. We have the best coach who will guide our every step. Even though we will misstep, we are told to "forget what is behind, and strain toward what is ahead. Press on

---

[1] 1 CORINTHIANS 9:24–27.

[2] HEBREWS 12:1–2.

toward the goal to win the prize for which God has called us heavenward in Christ Jesus."[3]

Teammate, press on! "You need to persevere so that when you have done the will of God, you will receive what he promised."[4] Remember, "No discipline seems pleasant at the time, but painful. Later on, however, it produces a harvest of righteousness and peace for those who have been trained by it."[5]

---

[3] PHILIPPIANS 3:13–14.

[4] HEBREWS 10:36.

[5] HEBREWS 12:11.

CHAPTER 17

QUIET LIFE

ADORATION

Praise God for his names, titles, and attributes that begin with *Q*.

Praise God for his invisible *qualities*.

> For since the creation of the world God's invisible qualities—his eternal power and divine nature—have been clearly seen, being understood from what has been made, so that people are without excuse.
> —ROMANS 1:20

Praise God! He is our *qualifier*.

> Joyfully give thanks to the Father, who has qualified you to share in the inheritance of the saints in the kingdom of light.
> —COLOSSIANS 1:12

Praise God! He is the one who *quenches* thirst.

> He makes the springs pour water into the ravines; he quenches their thirst.
> —PSALM 104:11

PAUSE AND ADORE HIM.

CONFESSION

This is what the Sovereign LORD, the Holy One of Israel, says: "in repentance and rest is your salvation; in quietness and trust is your strength, but you would have none of it."
—ISAIAH 30:15

Father, forgive me for the times I wanted none of you. "Be pleased to save me Lord; come quickly, LORD, to help me" (PSALM 40:13).

Turn your ear to me; come quickly to my rescue; be my rock of refuge, a strong fortress to save me.
—Psalm 31:2

Pause and confess your sins.

Thanksgiving

Joyfully give thanks to the Father, who has qualified you to share in the inheritance of the saints in the kingdom of light. For he has rescued us from the dominion of darkness and brought us into the kingdom of the Son he loves, in whom we have redemption, the forgiveness of sins.
—Colossians 1:12

It is good to wait quietly for the salvation of the Lord.
—Lamentations 3:26

Pause and thank him.

Supplication

Father God, I ask "supplications, prayers, intercessions, and thanksgiving be made for _____, that _____ may lead a peaceful and quiet life, godly and dignified in every way" (1 Timothy 2:1–2 ESV).

I pray _____ will be "quick to listen, slow to speak, slow to anger; for the anger of man does not bring about the righteous life that God desires" (James 1:19).

May _____ know that "the fruit of righteousness will be peace; the effect of righteousness will be quietness and confidence forever" (Isaiah 32:17).

Pray for those whose name begins with *Q*.

REFLECTION

David Teems, author, musician, and my editor, penned the words, *"May all that has been reduced to noise in you become music again."*[1] Approaching this quote with the same methodology I employ when studying the Bible, I read it again and then asked myself three questions. What does it say? What does it mean? What does it mean by way of application?

Being more left-brained than right, I often struggle to find meaning in poetry. It took contemplation to unpack his saying. What it signifies to me is that our lives have been reduced to noise. There is the constant bombardment of pings, dings, and buzzes. The noise can cause unrest often without our even realizing it. Regardless of the volume, it is distracting. Even as I type, there are the soft sounds of keyboard clacking and the air conditioner humming, along with the loud rumbling of trucks, the roar of engines, and the constant pounding of pilings from a nearby construction site.

It is easy to grow accustomed to the cacophony and be numbed by the relentless clamor. We get caught up in the reverberations and do not realize we are missing the most beautiful symphony of all.

The magnum opus is revealed in God's Holy Word and his creation.[2] In order to hear the song, we must unplug from the noise and be quiet. ZECHARIAH 2:13 states, "Be still before the LORD, all mankind, because he has roused himself from his holy dwelling."

The Maestro is awake. He is ready to lead, guide, and direct us in the most wonderfully orchestrated love song of our lives if we will pay attention and listen. First, we must be quiet.

Stop the noise. Listen to the music. Hear God and nature sing. It is beautiful!

---

[1] David Teems, To LOVE IS CHRIST, (Thomas Nelson/Harper Collins), 2005.

[2] PSALM 19; JOHN 1:14; ROMANS 1:19–25; 1 CORINTHIANS 2:10–15.

CHAPTER 18

RESOLVED

ADORATION

Praise God for his names, titles, and attributes that begin with *R*.

Praise God! He *rules*.

> Praise God, the blessed and only Ruler, the King of kings and Lord of lords.
> —1 TIMOTHY 6:15

Praise God! He *reigns*.

> The Lord reigns forever.
> —PSALM 9:7

Praise God! He is our *Rock*.

> He is the Rock, his works are perfect, and all his ways are just. A faithful God who does no wrong, upright and just is he.
> —DEUTERONOMY 32:4

Praise God! He is our *Redeemer*.

> Our Redeemer—the LORD Almighty is his name—is the Holy One of Israel.
> —ISAIAH 47:4

> They remembered that God was their Rock, that God Most High was their Redeemer.
> —PSALM 78:35

Praise God! He is our *refuge*.

> God is our refuge and strength, a very present help in trouble.
> —PSALM 46:1

Praise God! He is *righteous*.

> O LORD, God of Israel, you are righteous!
> —EZRA 9:15

Praise God! He is the *resurrection*.

> Jesus said, "I am the resurrection and the life."
> —JOHN 11:25

Praise God! His is a *revealer*.

> Surely your God is the God of gods and the Lord of kings
> and a revealer of mysteries.
> —DANIEL 2:47

Praise God! He is the *radiance* of God's glory.

> The Son is the radiance of God's glory and the exact repre-
> sentation of his being, sustaining all things by his powerful
> word.
> —HEBREWS 1:3

Praise God! He is the *rock*.

> May the words of my mouth and the mediation of my heart be
> pleasing in your sight, O LORD, my Rock and my Redeemer.
> —PSALM 19:14

PAUSE AND ADORE HIM.

CONFESSION

> This is what the Sovereign LORD says: "Repent! Turn from your
> idols and renounce all your detestable practices."
> —EZEKIEL 14:6

PAUSE AND CONFESS YOUR SINS.

THANKSGIVING

Jesus said to her, "I am the resurrection and the life. He who believes in me will live, even though he dies; and whoever lives and believes in me will never die."
—JOHN 11:25–26

PAUSE AND THANK HIM.

SUPPLICATION

O Lord, my Rock and Redeemer, I pray that _____ will be like Daniel and "resolve not to defile himself/herself" (DANIEL 1:8).

May _____ be devoted to godly principles and determined to do what is right in your sight, not giving in to the pressures around him/her.

Help _____ stand when trials and temptations come. I humbly ask you to strengthen and encourage _____ by the power of your Holy Spirit so _____ may live out his/her Christian convictions.

I trust in Your Word that states no one "will be tempted beyond what he can bear. But when tempted, you will provide a way out so that _____ can stand up under it" (1 CORINTHIANS 10:13).

PRAY FOR THOSE WHOSE NAME BEGINS WITH *R*.

REFLECTION

> *When all is said and done, the life of faith is nothing if*
> *not an unending struggle of spirit with every available*
> *weapon against the flesh.*
> —Dietrich Bonhoeffer, THE COST OF DISCIPLESHIP

Sex. Drugs. Alcohol. Pornography. These words were spoken often to our young sons. One day my son emphatically said, "Mom, please no more talks on sex, drugs, alcohol, and pornography!"

As their parent, it was my duty to warn our sons of worldly dangers and the pitfalls they could face. I felt compelled to let them know that sex outside of marriage, misuse of drugs, under-age consumption and overuse of alcohol, and pornography are actions condemned in Scripture. These sinful activities affect one's relationship with God and man, and often they have painful consequences.

Along with this message, I had our sons memorize the following passage from Corinthians.

> *Do you not know that your body is a temple of the Holy*
> *Spirit, who is in you, whom you have received from God?*
> *You are not your own; you were bought with a price.*
> *Therefore, honor God with your body.*
> —1 CORINTHIANS 6:19

Honoring God with their bodies meant our sons needed to be cognizant of what they allowed to enter into their hearts, minds, and mouths. I encouraged our sons to consider the content of books they read; the lyrics of the music they listened to; the language and scenes of the programs and movies they watched; and the food and drink they consumed. They were not to dishonor their bodies but treat "the temple" God had given them with respect because it is within their bodies that the Holy Spirit makes his dwelling.[1]

I often prayed my boys would be like Daniel and resolve not to defile themselves. I tried to warn them of coming dangers so they would know how to respond with resolve, to do what was right, and not give in to the peer pressures around them. I told them often, "Flee! Don't flirt with sin!" The Bible warns temptations will come.

> *No temptation has seized you except what is common to man. And God is faithful; he will not let you be tempted beyond what you can bear. But when you are tempted, he will also provide a way out so that you can stand up under it.*
> —1 CORINTHIANS 10:13

Warning our sons of present dangers and equipping them with the word of God was my duty. It was theirs, and still is to this day, to fight with the weapons God has given them—his Word and his Spirit.

Soldier of Christ, resolve not to defile yourself. Wield the sword of the Spirit and fight with every available weapon God has given you. Power resides in the person of Christ. Call on his mighty name. And know that in Jesus Christ, the victory is won!

> *Fight the good fight of the faith.*
> —1 TIMOTHY 6:12

---

[1] JOHN 14; 1 CORINTHIANS 3:16; 2 CORINTHIANS 6:16; ROMANS 8:9, 11.

CHAPTER 19

SPIRIT FILLED

ADORATION

Praise God for his names, titles, and attributes that begin with *S*.

Praise God! He is *sovereign*.

> How great you are, O Sovereign LORD! There is no one like you, and there is no God but you.
> —2 SAMUEL 7:22

Praise God! He is our *strength*.

> The Sovereign LORD is my strength.
> —HABAKKUK 3:19

Praise God! He is our *salvation*.

> The LORD lives, and blessed be my rock, and exalted be the God of my salvation.
> —PSALM 18:46 ESV

> Salvation belongs to our God who sits on the throne, and to the Lamb!
> —REVELATION 7:10

Praise God! He is our good *shepherd*.

> The LORD is my shepherd.
> —PSALM 23:1

Praise God! He is our *shelter*.

> For in the day of trouble he will keep me safe in his dwelling; he will hide me in the shelter of his tabernacle and set me high upon a rock.
> —PSALM 27:5

Praise God! He is our *shade*.

> The LORD is your shade on your right hand.
> —PSALM 121:5

Praise God! He is our *Savior*.

> My soul magnifies the Lord, and my spirit rejoices in God
> my Savior.
> —LUKE 1:47

Praise God! He is *spirit*.

> God is spirit, and his worshipers must worship in spirit and
> in truth.
> —JOHN 4:24

PAUSE AND ADORE HIM.

CONFESSION

> We have sinned, we have done wrong, we have acted wickedly.
> —1 KINGS 8:47

> Help us, O God our Savior, for the glory of your name; deliver
> us and forgive our sins for your name's sake!
> —PSALM 79:9

PAUSE AND CONFESS YOUR SINS.

THANKSGIVING

> He saved us, not because of works done by us in righteousness,
> but according to his own mercy, by the washing of regeneration
> and the renewal of the Holy Spirit.
> —TITUS 3:5 ESV

PAUSE AND THANK HIM.

SUPPLICATION

Spirit of the Living God, just as You chose Bezalel, please choose _____ and "fill him/her with the Spirit of God, with skill, ability and knowledge in all kinds of crafts" (Exodus 31:1–3).

Please give _____ an obedient heart to carry out all the work You give him/her to do and may he/she "do the work just as the Lord has commanded" (Exodus 36:1).

PRAY FOR THOSE WHOSE NAME BEGINS WITH *S*.

REFLECTION

Charles Ronald Payne, a successful small-town businessman, was a humble man of God. Prior to his death, his pastor told the children of his church, if one wants to know what Jesus was like, spend time with Ronnie Payne. He exuded love, joy, peace, patience, kindness, goodness, gentleness, faithfulness, and self-control.[1] Ronnie was indwelt with the Holy Spirit. He was led by the Spirit and lived by the Spirit. Ronnie's life was so full of the Spirit that the Fruit of the Spirit[2] was the passage his wife, my aunt, chose for his funeral service.

Scripture teaches about and distinguishes between the indwelling of the Holy Spirit and the filling of the Holy Spirit. The indwelling of the Spirit comes to everyone who admits to God he is a sinner, asks for forgiveness of his sin, believes Jesus is his Savior, and confesses with his mouth that Christ is Lord. This is without exception.[3] The indwelling of the Spirit comes at the moment of salvation. At

---

[1] GALATIANS 5:22–23.

[2] Ibid.

[3] JOHN 7:38–39.

that very moment, Christ sets his seal of ownership on the believer.[4] This condition is permanent.

The filling of the Holy Spirit is quite different. *"Be filled with the Spirit."*[5], is a command and comes with submission to God's Word. Filling of the Holy Spirit is a result of obedience and is hindered by disobedience. Our disobedience actually grieves the Holy Spirit and impedes the receipt of blessings in our lives. Therefore, "Do not grieve the Holy Spirit of God, with whom you were sealed for the day of redemption. Get rid of all bitterness, rage and anger, brawling and slander, along with every form of malice. Be kind and compassionate to one another, forgiving each other, just as in Christ God forgave you" (EPHESIANS 4:30–32).

My friend, are you indwelt with the Holy Spirit of God? That is, have you asked God to forgive your sins and be your Savior? If not, stop now and pray, "Dear Lord Jesus, I know that I am a sinner, and I ask forgiveness for the ways I have transgressed your laws and grieved your heart. I believe Christ died for my sins and was the atoning sacrifice for my sins. I desire to turn from my sins and invite You to be Lord of my life. Holy Spirit, help me to trust in Jesus as my Savior and follow You as Lord. Amen."

If the Holy Spirit already dwells within you, then, as a saved sinner, ask God to forgive all the ways you have grieved the Holy Spirit. As my pastor, Conrad "Buster" Brown, often reminds us, we are like leaky buckets that daily need to go to God's throne of grace and ask for a fresh filling of his Holy Spirit. Pray, "Spirit of the Living God, fall fresh upon me. Help me to 'live by the Spirit, keep in step with the Spirit,'[6] and bear the fruit of the Spirit, so others see Jesus Christ in me. To the praise of your glorious name. Amen."

---

[4] 2 CORINTHIANS 1:22; EPHESIANS 4:30.

[5] EPHESIANS 5:18.

[6] GALATIANS 5:25.

CHAPTER 20

TRUST

ADORATION

Praise God for his names, titles, and attributes that begin with *T.*

Praise God! He is *trustworthy*.

> Your decrees are very trustworthy; holiness befits your house, O LORD, forevermore.
> —PSALM 93:5 ESV

> The works of his hands are faithful and just; all his precepts are trustworthy.
> —PSALM 111:7

Praise God! His word is *true*.

> For the word of the LORD is right and true; he is faithful in all he does.
> —PSALM 33:4

Praise God! He is *truthful*.

> God is truthful.
> —JOHN 3:33

Praise God! He is *thorough*.

> Your promises have been thoroughly tested; Your law is true; Your statutes are forever right.
> —PSALM 119:140; 142; 144

Praise God! He is our *teacher*.

> Teacher, we know that you are true and teach the way of God truthfully.
> —MATTHEW 22:16 ESV

Praise God! He is our *thirst quencher*.

> He satisfies the thirsty and fills the hungry with good things.
> —PSALM 107:9

Praise God! He is *tender*.

> Because of the tender mercy of our God, by which the rising sun will come to us from heaven to shine on those living in darkness and in the shadow of death, to guide our feet into the path of peace.
> —LUKE 1:78–79

PAUSE AND ADORE HIM.

CONFESSION

> Yet you know me, O LORD; you see me and test my thoughts about you.
> —JEREMIAH 12:3

PAUSE AND CONFESS YOUR SINS.

THANKSGIVING

> I will give thanks to the LORD because of his righteousness and will sing praise to the name of the LORD Most High.
> —PSALM 7:17

PAUSE AND THANK HIM.

Supplication

Triune God, I pray _____ will "trust in the Lord with all his/her heart and lean not on his/her own understanding. In all _____'s ways may he/she acknowledge you, and You will make his/her path straight" (Proverbs 3:5–6).

Pray for those whose name begins with *T.*

Reflection

Throughout my life, I have not understood many occurences like the premature deaths of my high school friend, a college boyfriend, my mother, and my friend's child. I often have not understood God's plan in unanswered prayers for healing, protection, reconciliation, and restoration.

When I lack understanding and am perplexed, I reflect on my life verse, "Trust in the Lord with all your heart and lean not on your own understanding; in all your ways acknowledge him, and he will make your paths straight."[1]

A good summation of the meaning "to trust in the Lord" is found in the acronym TRUST—Totally Relying Upon Scriptural Truth. We cannot rely on what we do not know. We must open the Bible. Scripture reveals God's nature—his loving, kind, faithful, merciful, just, and unchanging nature. Scripture states God's Word is truth,[2] and that none of his promises have ever failed.[3] Through Bible study, we gain knowledge of God, his will, and his divine providence. As we come to know God more fully, we find ourselves able to totally rely upon the Lord who is trustworthy.[4]

---

[1] Proverbs 3:5–6.

[2] John 17:17.

[3] 1 Kings 8:56–57; Numbers 23:19; Psalm 89:34.

[4] 2 Samuel 7:28; Psalm 9:10; John 14:1; Romans 15:13.

The truth remains; many of God's ways are incomprehensible.[5]

> *"For my thoughts are not your thoughts, neither are your*
> *ways my ways," declares the LORD. "As the heavens are*
> *higher than the earth, so are my ways higher than your*
> *ways and my thoughts than your thoughts."*
> —ISAIAH 55:8–9

How can we reconcile this incomprehensibility in our minds? As pastor and professor Dr. Mark Ross said, "Don't let what you don't know confuse you about what you do know." Even when we cannot understand or comprehend God's ways, we can trust the Lord's purpose and ultimate plan.[6] We can find solace in scriptural promises.[7] Confidence can rest in knowing our loving God, who is omniscient,[8] omnipotent,[9] and omnipresent,[10] is in control and has our good at heart.[11] His invisible hand of providence is at work. God promises to protect us,[12] lead us,[13] and give us peace[14] and rest[15] as we trust in him, our sovereign Lord.

So, my friend, always TRUST (Totally Rely Upon Scriptural Truth) and forever FROG (Fully Rely On God)!

---

[5] DEUTERONOMY 29:29; ECCLESIASTES 8:17; ROMANS 11:33–36.

[6] JEREMIAH 29:11–13.

[7] DEUTERONOMY 31:6.

[8] ISAIAH 40:13–14; 46:9–10; PSALM 139:1–4; 15–16; ROMANS 11:33; HEBREWS 4:13; 1 JOHN 3:20.

[9] JOB 11:7–11; 37:23; PSALM 33:6; 147:5; ISAIAH 44:24; JEREMIAH 32:17; ROMANS 1:16.

[10] ISAIAH 66:12; JEREMIAH 23:23–24; PSALM 11:4–5; 139:7–10; MATTHEW 6:6.

[11] JEREMIAH 29:11–13; ROMANS 8:28–30.

[12] PSALM 84:11.

[13] PROVERBS 3:5–6.

[14] JOHN 14:27.

[15] PSALM 4:8.

CHAPTER 21

UNDIVIDED HEART

ADORATION

Praise God for his names, titles, and attributes that begin with *U.*

Praise God! He is *ubiquitous.*

> Where can I go from your Spirit? Where can I flee from your presence? If I go up to the heavens, you are there; if I make my bed in the depths, you are there. If I rise on the wings of the dawn, if I settle on the far side of the sea, even there your hand will guide me, your right hand will hold me fast.
> —PSALM 139:7–10

> The eternal God is your refuge, and underneath are the everlasting arms.
> —DEUTERONOMY 33:27

Praise God! He *understands.*

> For God is manifold in understanding.
> —JOB 11:6 ESV

> Great is our LORD, and abundant in power; his understanding is beyond measure.
> —PSALM 147:5 ESV

> With God is wisdom and might; he has counsel and understanding.
> —JOB 12:13 ESV

> The unfolding of your words gives light; it imparts understanding to the simple.
> —PSALM 119:130 ESV

Praise God! He *upholds* all things.

> Behold, God is my helper; the LORD is the upholder of my life.
> —PSALM 54:4 ESV

Praise God! He is a God of *unity*.

> And he made know to us the mystery of his will according
> to his good pleasure, which he purposed in Christ, to be put
> into effect when the times reach their fulfillment—to bring
> all things in heaven and on earth together under one head,
> even Christ.
> —EPHESIANS 1:8–10

Praise God! He is *unchanging*.

> I the LORD do not change.
> —MALACHI 3:6

PAUSE AND ADORE HIM.

CONFESSION

> So I find this law at work: When I want to do good, evil is right
> there with me. For in my inner being I delight in God's law; but I
> see another law at work in the members of my body, waging war
> against the law of my mind and making me a prisoner of the law
> of sin at work within me. What a wretched man I am!
> —ROMANS 7:21–24

PAUSE AND CONFESS YOUR SINS.

THANKSGIVING

> Who will rescue me from this body of death? Thanks be to
> God—through Jesus Christ our Lord!
> —ROMANS 7:24–25

PAUSE AND THANK HIM.

SUPPLICATION

Eternal God, I pray that _____ will "serve you with whole-hearted devotion and with a willing mind. May _____ understand that You search every heart and understand every motive behind the thoughts" (1 CHRONICLES 28:9).

"Teach _____ your way, O Lord, that he/she will walk in your truth; give _____ an undivided heart, that he/she may fear your name" (PSALM 86:11).

PRAY FOR THOSE WHOSE NAME BEGINS WITH *U*.

REFLECTION

Teach me your way, O Lord, and I will walk in your truth;
give me an undivided heart, that I may fear your name.
—PSALM 86:11

Our spiritual hearts are often like our chambered physical ones—divided. Although our physical heart is designed to be that way, our spiritual heart is not. The "undivided heart"[1] is a united heart. It has singleness of purpose. In the context of PSALM 86, the purpose is to revere God; however, we do not revere God as we ought. We are guilty of placing our desires and ourselves upon the throne of our heart rather than God.

I recall Tim Keller saying, "Our hearts are idol-making factories." I used to think of an idol as a golden calf. When commanded not to have any idols in my life, I thought, "I don't have anything like a golden calf in my life." Later, I realized an idol is anything I place before God.

---

[1] PSALM 86:11.

Our families, especially our spouses and our children, can be idols. Our possessions, work, recreation, and affiliation can be idols. A deeper look at our check registers or credit card statements can reveal idols in our lives. When we "make good gifts from God ultimate in our lives, thereby replacing God in our affections,"[2] they become idols.

"What is an idol? It is anything more important to you than God, anything that absorbs your heart and imagination more than God, anything you seek to give you what only God can give. ... A counterfeit god is anything so central and essential to your life that, should you lose it, your life would feel hardly worth living."[3]

Have you ever considered whether or not you have idols in your life? Ask yourself what in your life, if lost, would make life hardly worth living. Strive to put those things in their proper place and put God on the throne of your heart.

---

[2] Trevin Wax, "Counterfeit Gods: Tim Keller Takes On Our Idols," The Gospel Coalition, October 13, 2009.

[3] Tim Keller, Counterfiet Gods: The empty Promises of Money, Sex, and Power, and the Only Hope that Matters, (Penguin, 2009), xvii.

CHAPTER 22

VOICE

ADORATION

Praise God for his names, titles, and attributes that begin with *V*.

Praise God for his *voice*.

> The voice of the LORD is powerful; the voice of the LORD is majestic.
> —PSALM 29:4

Praise God! He is *victorious*.

> Now this I know: The LORD gives victory to his anointed. He answers him from his heavenly sanctuary with the victorious power of his right hand.
> —PSALM 20:6

Praise God! He is our *vindicator*.

> They will receive blessing from the LORD and vindication from God their Savior.
> —PSALM 24:5

Praise God for his *vastness*.

> How precious to me are your thoughts, O God! How vast is the sum of them!
> —PSALM 139:17

Praise God! He is the *vine*.

> I am the true vine, and my Father is the Gardener.
> —JOHN 15:1

Praise God! *Vengeance* is his.

For we know him who said, "Vengeance is mine, I will repay." And again, "The Lord will judge his people."
—HEBREWS 10:30 ESV

PAUSE AND ADORE HIM.

CONFESSION

Lord, we are sinful people who often possess "unbelieving hearts that turn away from the living God" (HEBREWS 3:12).

We hear but do not understand; see but do not perceive. For our hearts have become callous, and we hardly hear with our ears and we close our eyes (MATTHEW 13–15).

Forgive us when we are unresponsive and have "received God's grace in vain" (2 CORINTHIANS 6:1).

PAUSE AND CONFESS YOUR SINS.

THANKSGIVING

Thanks be to God, who gives us the victory through our Lord Jesus Christ.
—1 CORINTHIANS 15:57

PAUSE AND THANK HIM.

SUPPLICATION

Today, Lord, may _____ "hear Your voice, and not harden his/her heart" (HEBREWS 4:7).

"Morning by morning," awaken _____'s ear to hear as one being taught" (ISAIAH 50:4).

For the wise hear and increase in learning, and the one who understands obtains guidance.
—PROVERBS 1:5

PRAY FOR THOSE WHOSE NAME BEGINS WITH *V.*

REFLECTION

> *When God speaks, he does not give new revelation about himself that contradicts what he has already revealed in Scripture. Rather, God speaks to give application of his Word to the specific circumstances in your life. When God speaks to you, he is not writing a new book of Scripture; rather, he is applying to your life what he has already said in his Word.*
> —Henry T. Blackaby, HEARING GOD'S VOICE

The Bible records incidences of God's speaking to his people through different means. He used natural phenomena to speak to Elijah in "a gentle whisper."[1] John records his thunderous voice coming from heaven.[2] Moses heard God through an earthquake;[3] Job, in a storm.[4] Earthquakes, thunder, lightning, and whirlwinds have all been means by which the Lord has communicated with his people.

The Lord also spoke to the people through the prophets. He used them to speak the very words of God and teach in his name. Over one thousand times the Bible records the prophets saying, "the Lord said."

---

[1] 1 Kings 19:12.

[2] JOHN 12:28–29.

[3] EXODUS 19:16–19.

[4] JOB 38:1; JOB 37:1.

In the past God spoke to our forefathers through the prophets at many times and in various ways, but in these last day he has spoken to us by his Son.
—HEBREWS 1:1–2

Scripture says, "no prophecy of Scripture came about by the prophet's own interpretation. For prophecy never had its origin in the will of man, but men spoke from God as they were carried along by the Holy Spirit."[5]

When Jesus Christ, incarnate God, became flesh, he spoke the very words of God. After the crucifixion, resurrection, and ascension of Jesus, the Holy Spirit remained as our Helper or Counselor to speak to us.[6] Men under inspiration of the Holy Spirit wrote "God-breathed"[7] words for our instruction.

God has spoken. Are you listening? Are you applying to your life what God has said in his Word? Jesus said, "He who has ears, let him hear."[8] Purposely posture yourselves to hear from the Lord and say with Samuel, "Speak, Lord, for your servant is listening."[9]

[5] 2 PETER 1:20–21.

[6] JOHN 16:7.

[7] 2 TIMOTHY 3:16.

[8] MATTHEW 13:9.

[9] 1 SAMUEL 3:9–10.

CHAPTER 23

WALK IN YOUR WAY

ADORATION

Praise God for his names, titles, and attributes that begin with *W*.

Praise God! He is the *Word*.

> In the beginning was the Word, and the Word was with God, and the Word was God. He was in the beginning with God.
> —JOHN 1:1

> Your word is truth.
> —JOHN 17:17

Praise God! He is the *warrior*.

> The LORD is with me like a mighty warrior.
> —JEREMIAH 20:11

Praise God! He is the *watchman*.

> For the LORD watches over the way of the righteous.
> —PSALM 1:6

> From his dwelling place He watches all who live on earth.
> —PSALM 33:14

> He who watches over Israel will neither slumber nor sleep.
> —PSALM 121:4

> The LORD watches over all who love him.
> —PSALM 145:20

Praise God! He is the living *water*.

> Everyone who drinks this water will be thirsty again, but whoever drinks the water I give him will never thirst. Indeed, the water I give him will become in him a spring of water welling up to eternal life.
> —JOHN 4:14

Praise God! He is the *way*.

> Jesus said to him, "I am the way, the truth, and the life. No one comes to the Father except through me."
> —JOHN 14:6

Praise God! He is *wonderful* and *wise*.

> The LORD Almighty is wonderful in counsel and magnificent in wisdom.
> —ISAIAH 28:29

Praise God! He is *worthy*.

> Worthy is the Lamb who was slain, to receive power and wealth and wisdom and might and honor and glory and blessing!
> —REVELATION 5:12

PAUSE AND ADORE HIM.

CONFESSION

> The heart is deceitful above all things and beyond cure. Who can understand it?
> —JEREMIAH 17:9

> But you do not realize you are wretched, pitiable, poor, blind and naked.
> —REVELATION 3:17

Wash the evil from your heart and be saved. How long will you harbor wicked thoughts?
—JEREMIAH 4:14

Repent of this wickedness and pray to the Lord. Perhaps he will forgive you for having such a thought in your heart.
—ACTS 8:22

PAUSE AND CONFESS YOUR SINS.

THANKSGIVING

For in Christ all the fullness of the Deity lives in bodily form, and you have been given fullness in Christ, who is the head over every power and authority. In him you were also circumcised, in the putting off of the sinful nature, not with a circumcision done by the hands of men but with the circumcision done by Christ, having been buried with him in baptism and raised with him through your faith in the power of God, who raised him from the dead. When you were dead in your sins and in the uncircumcision of your sinful nature, God made you alive with Christ. He forgave us all our sins, having canceled the written code, with its regulations, that was against us and that stood opposed to us; he took it away, nailing it to the cross. And having disarmed the powers and authorities, he made a public spectacle of them, triumphing over them by the cross.
—COLOSSIANS 2:9–15

PAUSE AND THANK HIM.

SUPPLICATION

Who is wise? He will realize these things. Who is discerning? He will understand them. The ways of the LORD are right; the righteous walk in them, but the rebellious stumble in them.
—HOSEA 14:9

Lord, I pray for _____ to "walk in Your way and not set foot on the path of the wicked or walk in the way of evil men. Help _____ avoid it, and not travel on it; to turn from it and go Your way" (PROVERBS 4:14–15).

Holy Spirit, guide _____ down the path of righteousness so that he/she may be like "the first gleam of dawn, shining ever brighter till the full light of day" (PROVERBS 4:18).

PRAY FOR THOSE WHOSE NAME BEGINS WITH *W*.

REFLECTION

A frequent prayer of mine for our sons is for them to "show themselves to be men who walk in God's way."[1] Based on King David's charge to Solomon, this father exhorted his son to keep God's laws central to his private and public life.

As a fearless young man,[2] David loved God's law.[3] He trusted, obeyed, and faithfully relied upon him, so much so that David became known as "a man after God's own heart."[4] Yet, this dedicated man of God committed the heinous sins of adultery and murder.

How could a godly man commit such grievous sins? David sinned when he strayed off of the path of faithful obedience to God. His failure to stay in close proximity with God had rippling effects resulting in much grief, pain, and suffering. His experiences taught him fortitude was needed to walk in faithful obedience to the Lord. Hence, David's opening words to Solomon—*Be strong!*

---

[1] 1 KINGS 2:2–4.

[2] 1 SAMUEL 17.

[3] PSALM 119:47–48.

[4] ACTS 13:22.

The strength that this dying, warrior king encouraged his son to have came, paradoxically, not by mettle but by surrender, surrender to God's Word and obedience to God's ways.

Like David, we are "prone to wander, prone to leave the God we love."[5] Therefore, we must beseech the Holy Spirit to empower us to follow David's charge, "be strong, show yourself a man, and observe what the LORD your God requires: Walk in his ways, and keep his decrees and commands, his laws and requirements, as written in the Law of Moses, so that you may prosper in all you do and wherever you go…"[6]

---

[5] Robert Robertson, "Come Thou Fount of Every Blessing," 1758.

[6] 1 KINGS 2:2–4.

CHAPTER 24

EXCEL IN EVERYTHING

ADORATION

Praise God for his names, titles, and attributes that begin with *X*. *Ex*-ceptions are being made for *X*.

Praise God! *Exalt* the Lord!

> Oh, magnify the LORD with me, and let us exalt his name together!
> —PSALM 34:3 ESV

> Yours, O LORD is the greatness and the power and the glory and the victory and the majesty, for all that is in the heavens and in the earth is yours. Yours is the kingdom, O LORD, and you are exalted as head above all.
> —1 CHRONICLES 29:11 ESV

Praise God! He is *excellent*.

> He is wonderful in counsel and excellent in wisdom.
> —ISAIAH 28:29 ESV

> Praise him for his mighty deeds; praise him according to his excellent greatness!
> —PSALM 150:2 ESV

Praise God! Jesus "is the radiance of the glory of God and the *exact* imprint of his nature, and he upholds the universe by the word of his power" (HEBREWS 1:3 ESV).

Praise God for Christ's *example*!

> For to this you have been called, because Christ also suffered for you, leaving you an example, so that you might follow in his steps.
> —1 PETER 2:21 ESV

PAUSE AND ADORE HIM.

CONFESSION

> Examine yourselves to see whether you are in the faith. Test yourselves.
> —2 CORINTHIANS 13:5

PAUSE AND CONFESS YOUR SINS.

THANKSGIVING

> Have this mind among yourselves, which is yours in Christ Jesus, who, though he was in the form of God, did not count equality with God a thing to be grasped, but emptied himself, by taking the form of a servant, being born in the likeness of men. And being found in human form, he humbled himself by becoming obedient to the point of death, even death on a cross. Therefore God has highly exalted him and bestowed on him the name that is above every name, so that at the name of Jesus every knee should bow, in heaven and on earth and under the earth, and every tongue confess that Jesus Christ is Lord, to the glory of God the Father.
> —PHILIPPIANS 2:5–11 ESV

PAUSE AND THANK HIM.

SUPPLICATION

Lord, I pray _____ will "excel in everything—in faith, in speech, in knowledge, in complete earnestness and in love. May _____ also excel in the grace of giving" (2 CORINTHIANS 8:7).

PRAY FOR THOSE WHOSE NAME BEGINS WITH *X*.

REFLECTION

Do your best! Reach for the stars! Be the best you that you can be! These motivational statements are generally used to encourage self-promotion in order to gain personal recognition, power, wealth, or status.

The apostle Paul had another purpose in mind when he encouraged the Corinthians to "excel in everything."[1] The goal was not for personal advancement and self-aggrandizement but to advance the kingdom of God and to bring glory to his holy name through the grace of giving.

God created each person skillfully, thoughtfully, and purposefully in his image.[2] The Bible says, "we are God's workmanship created in Christ Jesus to do good works, which God prepared in advance for us to do."[3] God graciously bestowed on each person unique gifts, talents, and abilities in order to build up his church. He blesses his people in order that they might be a blessing. Paul said we have been "made rich in every way so that we can be generous on every occasion."[4]

---

[1] 2 CORINTHIANS 8:7.

[2] GENESIS 1:27.

[3] EPHESIANS 2:10.

[4] 2 CORINTHIANS 9:11.

To be "rich in every way" means more than money. Our "faith, speech, and knowledge"[5] can bless others. Time can be given to those in need; compassion, to the hurting; and encouragement, to the discouraged. When done in love, using our gifts to bless others demonstrates our faith.

Beloved, what are you doing with the gifts God gave you? Are you striving to "excel in everything" for God's glory or for your own personal gain? Let us acknowledge all that we have and all that we are is a gift from our Heavenly Father.[6] A. W. Tozer said, "Refuse to be average. Let your heart soar as high as it will."[7] Do all things out of love and devotion to God, to the glory and praise of his most excellent name.

[5] 2 CORINTHIANS 8:7.

[6] JAMES 1:17–18.

[7] Attributed to A. W. Tozer.

CHAPTER 25

YEARN FOR THE LORD

ADORATION

Praise God for his names, titles, and attributes that begin with *Y.*

In the Old Testament, the Hebrew word for "God" is *Elohim*. God is also called "LORD," which translates *Adonai*. However, the special name of God that is given in EXODUS 3:14 is YHWH, which is "I AM."

Praise *Yahweh*! The Great "I AM"!

And God said to Moses, "I AM WHO I AM."
—EXODUS 3:14

I am God, and there is no other; I am God, and there is none like me.
—ISAIAH 46:9

I am God Almighty.
—GENESIS 17:1

I am the LORD; that is my name! I will not give my glory to another or my praise to idols.
—ISAIAH 42:8

I am the LORD, and apart from me there is no savior. I am he.
—ISAIAH 43:11;13

I the LORD do not change.
—MALACHI 3:6

Yours, O LORD, is the greatness and the power and the glory and the splendor, for everything in heaven and earth is yours. Yours, O LORD, is the kingdom; you are exalted as head over all.
—1 CHRONICLES 29:11

PAUSE AND ADORE HIM.

CONFESSION

Come, my people, enter your chambers, and shut your doors behind you; hide yourselves for a little while until the fury has passed by. For behold, the LORD is coming out from his place to punish the inhabitants of the earth for their iniquity.
—ISAIAH 26:20–21 ESV

PAUSE AND CONFESS YOUR SINS.

THANKSGIVING

Come and hear, all you who fear God, and I will tell what he has done for my soul. I cried to him with my mouth, and high praise was on my tongue. If I had cherished iniquity in my heart, the Lord would not have listened. But truly God has listened; he has attended to the voice of my prayer. Blessed be God, because he has not rejected my prayer or removed his steadfast love from me!
—PSALM 66:16–20 ESV

PAUSE AND THANK HIM.

SUPPLICATION

Great I AM, may "your name and renown be the desire of _____'s heart. May his/her soul yearn for You in the night; in the morning may_____'s spirit long for You" (ISAIAH 26:8–9).

PRAY FOR THOSE WHOSE NAME BEGINS WITH Y.

REFLECTION

You made us for yourself, O Lord, and our hearts are restless until they rest in you.
—St. Augustine, CONFESSIONS

The students affectionately knew Isla Montague McMillan, Professor Emerita, Limestone College, as Dr. Mac. As fitting for an English professor, she was wise with her words and had a profound influence upon her students. One such student was my mother, whom she affectionately called Little Miss Nell. The two shared a close relationship their entire lives.

As intimate friends, my mother shared with Dr. Mac some of the longings of her heart. Knowing my mother to be a person of faith and prayer, Dr. Mac often responded, "Little Miss Nell, be careful what you pray for. You're apt to get it."

The yearnings of our heart are inescapable. God places longings there for the purpose of drawing us into a close relationship with him. It has been said, "There is a God-shaped vacuum in the heart of each man which cannot be satisfied by any created thing but only by God the Creator, made known through Jesus Christ."[1]

When created things become ultimate things or idols in our lives, we seek them with all our heart; yet they cannot satisfy. As Derek Thomas said, "Getting what our hearts dream of could be our greatest undoing. Why? Because our hearts dream of less than they should. We were made to glorify God, but our hearts dream of self-glory."[2]

For what are you yearning? Are you longing for things of this world? Do you dream of self-glory? Are your prayers for your will

---

[1] Attributed to Blaise Pascal.

[2] Derek W. H. Thomas, STRENGTH FOR THE WEARY, (Reformation Trust Publishing, 2018), 52.

to be done, rather than "Thy will be done?"[3] Making a right relationship with God our utmost priority and pursuing his desires for
our lives is where you will find rest and satisfaction. Jesus promised
when we "seek first the kingdom of God and his righteousness, and
all these things will be added to you."[4]

---

[3] MATTHEW 6:10.

[4] MATTHEW 6:33 ESV.

CHAPTER 26

ZEAL FOR THE LORD

ADORATION

Praise God for his names, titles, and attributes that begin with **Z**.

Praise God! He is *zealous*!

> Sing to the LORD a new song, his praise from the ends of the earth, you who go down to the sea, and all that is in it, you islands, and all who live in them. Let the wilderness and its towns raise their voices; let the settlements where Kedar lives rejoice. Let the people of Sela sing for joy; let them shout from the mountaintops. Let them give glory to the LORD and proclaim his praise in the islands. The LORD will march out like a champion, like a warrior he will stir up his zeal; with a shout he will raise the battle cry and will triumph over his enemies.
> —ISAIAH 42:10–13

> Therefore, this is what the Sovereign LORD says: I will restore the fortunes of Jacob and will have compassion on all the people of Israel, and I will be zealous for my holy name.
> —EZEKIEL 39:25

PAUSE AND ADORE HIM.

CONFESSION

This is what the Sovereign LORD says: "In my burning zeal I have spoken against the rest of the nations, and against all Edom, for with glee and with malice in their hearts they made my land their own possession so that they might plunder its pastureland."
—EZEKIEL 36:5

Again, the word of the LORD came to me: "Son of man, when the people of Israel were living in their own land, they defiled it by their conduct and their actions."
—EZEKIEL 36:17

PAUSE AND CONFESS YOUR SINS.

THANKSGIVING

I will sprinkle clean water on you, and you will be clean; I will cleanse you from all your impurities and from all your idols. I will give you a new heart and put a new spirit in you; I will remove from you your heart of stone and give you a heart of flesh. I will put my Spirit in you and move you to follow my decrees and be careful to keep my laws. I will save you from all your uncleanness.
—EZEKIEL 36:25–27, 29

PAUSE AND THANK HIM.

SUPPLICATION

Zealous God, by the power of your Holy Spirit, I pray that zeal for the Lord will consume _____. May "your commands be _____ 's delight" (PSALM 119:143).

I pray _____ will "never lack in zeal, but keep his/her spiritual fervor, serving the Lord" (ROMANS 12:11).

PRAY FOR THOSE WHOSE NAME BEGINS WITH **Z**.

REFLECTION

As a fifth grader, I looked with excitement to Friday nights when I could attend the high school standing-room-only basketball game to cheer from the stands for my brother's team. On one occasion, at the height of play, my enthusiasm got the best of me. Shrieking with fervor, the players thought a referee's whistle had blown. Play stopped! All eyes turned toward the stands. Expecting to see a whistle pursed between someone's lips, everyone was shocked to discover the sound was the high-pitched shrills of an over-zealous young girl.

Zeal is often thought of as extreme enthusiasm for something or some cause, like the eagerness I displayed as a fanatical fan. Biblical zeal can refer to excessive passion[1], but more often the Bible's Hebrew or Greek word for zeal has an entirely different meaning.

ISAIAH 9 portends the coming of the Messiah. The chapter foretells of the work our triune God will do—establish an eternal kingdom where Jesus will reign in righteousness. "The zeal of the LORD Almighty will accomplish this."[2] In this passage, the word "zeal" is *qin'a*, which means jealousy or envy.

God's zeal is born out of his revulsion at sin and out of his deep love for us as expressed in his act of redemption. God said we are not to make, bow down to, or worship idols, for "I, the LORD your God, am a jealous God."[3] God is jealous of those things that belong to him! His zeal is righteous. God bought us with a price,[4] the atoning sacrifice of his one and only Son.[5] God alone is worthy of all worship, honor, and praise.

---

[1] 2 SAMUEL 21:2; 2 CORINTHIANS 11:2.

[2] ISAIAH 9:8.

[3] EXODUS 20:5.

[4] 1 CORINTHIANS 6:20.

[5] 1 JOHN 4:10.

Like a husband who is jealous for the affections of his wife, "the LORD, whose name is Jealous"[6] is jealous for what is rightly due him. God's zeal for his own is not born out of weakness or fear but from a holy indignation of one's attention being given to someone or something rather than him.

To whom or what are you giving your attention? God's desire is for us to forsake all others and be zealous for him alone. May we not play the harlot but give our hearts to God making him our first love and soley cleave to him.

---

[6] EXODUS 34:14.

Section II

Prayers for the Fruit of the Spirit

CHAPTER 27

LOVE

ADORATION

Praise God! He is *love*.

Sow for yourselves righteousness, reap the fruit of unfailing love, and break up your unplowed ground; for it is time to seek the Lord.
—HOSEA 10:12

God is love.
—1 JOHN 4:8

Praise be to the LORD, for he showed his wonderful love to me.
—PSALM 31:21

By day the LORD directs his love, at night his song is with me—a prayer to the God of my life.
—PSALM 42:8

Put your hope in the LORD, for with the LORD is unfailing love and with him is full redemption.
—PSALM 130:7

But I trust in your unfailing love; my heart rejoices in your salvation. I will sing to the LORD, for he has been good to me.
—PSALM 13:5–6

The earth is full of his unfailing love.
—PSALM 33:5

How priceless is your unfailing love!
—PSALM 36:7

PAUSE AND ADORE HIM.

CONFESSION

But mark this: There will be terrible times in the last days. People will be lovers of themselves, lovers of money, boastful, proud, abusive, disobedient to their parents, ungrateful, unholy, without love, unforgiving, slanderous, without self-control, brutal, not lovers of the good, treacherous, rash, conceited, lovers of pleasure rather than lovers of God—having a form of godliness but denying its power.
—2 TIMOTHY 3:1–5

I have sinned. I violated the LORD's commands. Now I beg you forgive my sin so that I may worship the LORD.
—1 SAMUEL 15:24–25

PAUSE AND CONFESS YOUR SINS.

THANKSGIVING

Let them give thanks to the LORD for his unfailing love and his wonderful deeds for mankind.
—PSALM 107:8

For God so loved the world that he gave his one and only Son, that whoever believes in him shall not perish but have eternal life.
—JOHN 3:16

But because of his great love for us, God, who is rich in mercy, made us alive with Christ even when we were dead in transgressions—it is by grace you have been saved.
—EPHESIANS 2:4–5

Because of the LORD's great love we are not consumed, for his compassions never fail. They are new every morning; great is your faithfulness.
—LAMENTATIONS 3:22–23

Know therefore that the LORD your God is God; he is the faithful God, keeping his covenant of love to a thousand generations of those who love him and keep his commands.
—DEUTERONOMY 7:9

PAUSE AND THANK HIM.

SUPPLICATION

LORD of love, I pray _____ will "be an imitator of God, as a dearly loved child and live a life of love" (EPHESIANS 5:1–2).

May _____ be "patient and kind; may _____ not envy or boast or be proud. I pray that _____ will not be rude or self-seeking; that _____ will not be easily angered. I ask that you help _____ keep no record of wrongs. May _____ not delight in evil but rejoice with the truth. Fill _____ with agape love, which always protects, always trusts, always hopes, always perseveres" (1 CORINTHIANS 13:4–7).

PRAY FOR THOSE WHO NEED TO KNOW THE LOVE OF CHRIST.

REFLECTION

Love. What exactly is love? Is love an action? Is love a feeling? In English, the one word "love" conveys a multitude of meanings. Love is expressed in everything from love for food to love of God, though in vastly different ways. However, the Bible, written in Hebrew and Greek, uses four words to express or define love.

The four kinds of love found in the Bible are *Eros, Phileo, Storge,* and *Agape. Eros* is erotic or romantic love; the one-flesh love demonstrated in relationships, from a man "knowing" his wife to Judah's love for Tamar.[1] It is sexual love. *Phileo* is platonic love, like David

---

[1] GENESIS 38.

and Jonathan's.[2] It is the love of friends, brotherly love. *Storge* is natural, instinctual love, like the deep affection of a parent for a child. *Agape* is God's sacrificial, unconditional love demonstrated toward his children. It is his "steadfast love," his "lovingkindness."

Love is, therefore, an action and a feeling. It encompasses human affections; one's concern for another's well-being and one's commitment to sacrifice for another. Love's origin is in our triune God, within the eternal relationship that exists between God the Father, his Son and the Holy Spirit. In the highest sense, love is a commitment, an act of the will. "God demonstrated his own love for us in this: While we were still sinners, Christ died for us."[3]

> *Dear friends, let us love one another, for love comes from God...if we love one another, God lives in us and his love is made complete in us.... He gives us a command: Whoever loves God must also love his brother.*
> —1 JOHN 4:7, 12, 21

---

[2] 1 SAMUEL 18; 1 SAMUEL 20.

[3] ROMANS 5:8.

CHAPTER 28

JOY

ADORATION

Praise God for his *joy*!

> Shout with joy to God, all the earth! Sing the glory of his name; make his praise glorious!
> —PSALM 66:1

> Sing joyfully to the LORD, you righteous; it is fitting for the upright to praise him.
> —PSALM 33:1

> Splendor and majesty are before him; strength and joy in his dwelling place.
> —1 CHRONICLES 16:27

> Those living far away fear your wonders; where morning dawns and evening fades you call forth songs of joy.
> —PSALM 65:8

> The trees of the forest will sing, they will sing for joy before the LORD.
> —1 CHRONICLES 16:33

> The precepts of the LORD are right, giving joy to the heart. The commands of the LORD are radiant, giving light to the eyes.
> —PSALM 19:8

> The LORD is my strength and my shield; my heart trusts in him, and he helps me. My heart leaps for joy, and with my song I praise him.
> —PSALM 28:7

To him who is able to keep you from falling and to present you before his glorious presence without fault and with great joy—to the only God our Savior be glory, majesty, power and authority, through Jesus Christ our LORD, before all ages, now and forevermore! Amen.
—JUDE 24–25

PAUSE AND ADORE HIM.

CONFESSION

When anxiety was great within me, your consolation brought joy to my soul.
—PSALM 94:19

PAUSE AND CONFESS YOUR SINS.

THANKSGIVING

Let us sing for joy to the LORD; let us shout aloud to the Rock of our salvation.
—PSALM 95:1

You make known to me the path of life; you will fill me with joy in your presence, with eternal pleasures at your right hand.
—PSALM 16:11

The LORD has done great things for us, and we are filled with joy.
—PSALM 126:3

PAUSE AND THANK HIM.

SUPPLICATION

Father God, I pray "for the joy of the LORD to be _____ 's strength" (NEHEMIAH 8:10).

May _____ "take refuge in you and be glad; let _____ ever sing for joy. Spread your protection over _____, that he/she will love your name and rejoice in you" (PSALM 5:11).

"Fill _____ 's mouth with laughter and _____'s lips with shouts of joy" (JOB 8:21).

PRAY FOR THOSE WHO NEED TO KNOW THE JOY OF CHRIST.

REFLECTION

Marie Kondo, the de-cluttering guru, coined the phrase, "Does it spark joy?" Her advice is to get rid of all those things in life that weigh you down and keep only those things that bring joy. Though I have only seen a brief video clip of hers, I perceive her message to be "if you get rid of the mess and order your physical life, you will find joy." The problem is this type of joy is fleeting and will not last.

The message of the Bible is that only Jesus Christ and the indwelling of the Holy Spirit can give joy. Jesus tells us that joy is maintained by abiding in Christ. He said, "If you obey my commands, you will remain in my love, just as I have obeyed my Father's commands and remain in his love. I have told you this so that my joy may be in you and that your joy may be complete."[1]

In the day of Nehemiah, after the broken walls around Jerusalem were rebuilt, the Book of the Law was read. The people listened attentively to the message, repented of their sin, and renewed their

---

[1] JOHN 15:10–11.

commitment to the Lord. Nehemiah reminded them, "The joy of the LORD is your strength."[2]

The same is true today. Joy that comes from the world is fleeting, but everlasting joy comes from the Spirit of God.

And the ransomed of the LORD shall return and come to Zion with singing; everlasting joy shall be upon their heads; they shall obtain gladness and joy, sorrow and sighing shall flee away.
—ISAIAH 35:10 ESV

---

[2] NEHEMIAH 8:10.

CHAPTER 29

PEACE

ADORATION

Praise God! He is the *Prince of Peace.*

> He will be called Wonderful Counselor, Mighty God, Everlasting Father, Prince of Peace.
> —ISAIAH 9:6

Praise God! He is the One who promises *peace.*

> I will listen to what God the LORD will say; he promises peace to his people, his saints.
> —PSALM 85:8

Praise God! He gives *peace* in the Holy Spirit.

> For the kingdom of God is not a matter of eating and drinking, but of righteousness, peace, and joy in the Holy Spirit.
> —ROMANS 14:17

Praise God! He gives wisdom that leads to *peace.*

> The ways of wisdom are pleasant ways, and all wisdom's paths are peace.
> —PROVERBS 3:17

Praise God! The LORD is *Peace.* (JUDGES 6:24)

> You know the message God sent to the people of Israel, announcing the good news of peace through Jesus Christ, who is Lord of all.
> —ACTS 10:36

Rejoice in the Lord always. I will say it again: Rejoice! Let your gentleness be evident to all. The Lord is near. Do not be anxious about anything, but in everything, by prayer and petition, with thanksgiving, present your requests to God. And the peace of God, which transcends all understanding, will guard your hearts and your minds in Christ Jesus.
—PHILIPPIANS 4:4–7

PAUSE AND ADORE HIM.

CONFESSION

I have no peace, no quietness; I have no rest, but only turmoil.
—JOB 3:26

PAUSE AND CONFESS YOUR SINS.

THANKSGIVING

Therefore, since we have been justified through faith, we have peace with God through our Lord Jesus Christ.
—ROMANS 5:1

PAUSE AND THANK HIM.

SUPPLICATION

Prince of Peace, I pray _____ will "make every effort to do what leads to peace and mutual edification" (ROMANS 14:19).

My God of hope, please fill _____ with "all joy and peace as he/she trusts in you, so that _____ may overflow with hope by the power of the Holy Spirit" (ROMANS 15:13).

Father, please "turn Your face toward _____ and give him/her peace" (NUMBERS 6:26).

PRAY FOR THOSE WHO NEED TO KNOW THE PEACE OF CHRIST.

REFLECTION

> *Because peace is a fruit of the Spirit, we are dependent upon the Spirit's work in our lives to produce the desire and the means to pursue peace. But we are also responsible to use the means He has given us and to take all practical steps to attain both peace within and peace with others.*[1]
> —Jerry Bridges, THE PRACTICE OF GODLINESS

What comes to mind when you think of peace? Is peace the absence of noise? Is peace tranquility? Is peace a lack of conflict? How is peace obtained?

In the Bible, peace is first mentioned in Genesis 15:15 where the Lord tells Abram, "you will go to your fathers in peace and be buried at a good old age. The Old Testament word for peace is *"shalom"*, which means completeness, harmony, and well-being. Shalom connotes security, safety, satisfaction, and contentment.

In Anglican, Catholic, or Episcopal church services you may have experienced the passing of peace. The priest states, "The peace of the Lord be always with you." The people respond, "And also with you." Congregrants then demonstrate accord with Christ and others with a handshake, hug, or kiss of peace. This liturgical exchange is a mere shadow of what God accomplished for sinners through Christ's atoning work on the cross.

Paul states, "Therefore, since we have been justified through faith, we have peace with God through our Lord Jesus Christ, through whom we have gained access by faith into this grace in which we now stand."[2] Peace is a gift from God.

---

[1] Jerry Bridges, THE PRACTICE OF GODLINESS, (NavPress, 1996), 166.

[2] ROMANS 5:1–2.

God's gift of peace allows one to have peace with God, inner peace, and peace with fellow man. Not only is peace a gift, but also a command. Peace must be pursued. Scripture states, "Make every effort to live in peace with all men, and to be holy."[3] In our relationships, we are commanded to, "Aim for restoration, comfort one another, agree with one another, live in peace."[4] This command is tied to the promise that "the God of love and peace will be with you."[5]

Are you at peace with God? Do you have peace within? Are you at peace with others? Are you actively pursuing peace in all relationships? Ask the God of peace to give you peace and fill you with the fruit of peace[6] as you trust in him.[7] Turmoil may abound, but peace can ensue because of God's gift of peace.[8]

You will keep in perfect peace him whose mind is steadfast, because he trusts you.
—ISAIAH 26:3

---

[3] HEBREWS 12:14.

[4] 2 CORINTHIANS 13:11 ESV.

[5] Ibid.

[6] GALATIANS 5:22.

[7] 2 THESSALONIANS 3:16

[8] JOHN 16:33.

CHAPTER 30

PATIENCE

ADORATION

Praise God! He is *patient.*

> The LORD, the LORD, the compassionate and gracious God, is slow to anger and abounding in love and faithfulness.
> —EXODUS 34:6

> God waited patiently in the days of Noah while the ark was being built.
> —1 PETER 3:20

> The LORD is gracious and compassionate, slow to anger and rich in love.
> —PSALM 145:8

> The LORD is slow to anger and great in power.
> —NAHUM 1:3

> The fruit of the Spirit is … patience.
> —GALATIANS 5:22

> Love is patient.
> —1 CORINTHIANS 13:4

> For the LORD is good and his love endures forever; his faithfulness continues through all generations.
> —PSALM 100:5

PAUSE AND ADORE HIM.

CONFESSION

Do not forget this one thing, dear friends: With the Lord a day is like a thousand years, and a thousand years are like a day. The Lord is not slow in keeping his promises, as some understand slowness. He is patient with you, not wanting anyone to perish, but everyone to come to repentance.
—2 PETER 3:8–9

Father, you maintain love to thousands, and forgive wickedness, rebellion and sin. Yet you do not leave the guilty unpunished; you punish the children and their children for the sin of the fathers to the third and fourth generation (EXODUS 34:7).

Rend your heart and not your garments. Return to the LORD your God, for he is gracious and compassionate, slow to anger and abounding in love, and he relents from sending calamity.
—JOEL 2:13

PAUSE AND CONFESS YOUR SINS.

THANKSGIVING

But you are a forgiving God, gracious and compassionate, slow to anger and abounding in love.
—NEHEMIAH 9:17

PAUSE AND THANK HIM.

SUPPLICATION

Heavenly Father, your word says, "Better a patient man than a warrior, a man who controls his temper than one who takes a city" (PROVERBS 16:32).

A hot-tempered man stirs up conflict, but the one who is patient calms a quarrel.
—PROVERBS 15:18

God of grace, fill _____ with your Holy Spirit so that _____ will "be completely humble and gentle; be patient, bearing with others in love" (EPHESIANS 4:2).

May _____ "be joyful in hope, patient in affliction, faithful in prayer" (ROMANS 12:12).

PRAY FOR THOSE WHO NEED TO KNOW THE PATIENCE OF CHRIST.

REFLECTION

Patience is something all of us want but that virtue for which we cannot wait. In this age of instant gratification, the concept of patience is foreign. So, we pray, "Lord, give me patience now!"

"Biblical patience is a God-exercised, or God-given restraint in the face of opposition or oppression. It is not passivity. The initiative lies in God's love."[1] As noted in the Old Testament, patience is *long* or *slow*.

> The LORD, the LORD, the compassionate and gracious God,
> slow to anger, abounding in love and faithfulness.
> —EXODUS 34:6–7

The New Testament records the prophets "as an example of patience in the face of trials."[2] James specifically mentioned Job's perseverance[3] as a model of patience for us to emulate. Paul said that those who patiently persist in doing God's will receive eternal life.[4]

Throughout the Scriptures, it is recorded that God's patience has purpose, which is to bring about our salvation, sanctification, and

---

[1] NEW BIBLE DICTIONARY THIRD EDITION, (InterVarsity Press, 1996), 873.

[2] JAMES 5:10.

[3] JAMES 5:11.

[4] ROMANS 2:7.

glorification. "He is patient with you, not wanting anyone to perish, but everyone to come to repentance."[5]

R. Albert Mohler, Jr., said, "We must understand that patience is both a command and a gift from God... As a command, patience arrives at the Christian conscience as a matter of accountability. At the same time, patience is a divine gift. Christians are not able, in and of themselves, to demonstrate true patience as a fruit of the Spirit... [Patience] comes only to those who have been redeemed by Christ and in whom the Holy Spirit is calling forth the fruit of the Spirit."[6]

Redeemed of the Lord, have you asked the Holy Spirit to produce the fruit of patience in you? If not, pray for patience to grow in your life. Strive to show the same kindness and forbearance toward others that Christ has shown to you.

[5] 2 PETER 3:9.

[6] R. Albert Mohler, Jr., TABLETALK, (September 2004), 17–18.

CHAPTER 31

KINDNESS

ADORATION

Praise God for his *kindness*!

> I will tell of the kindnesses of the LORD, the deeds for which he is to be praised, according to all the LORD has done for us—yes, the many good things he has done according to his compassion and many kindnesses.
> —ISAIAH 63:7

> "I am the LORD, who exercises kindness, justice and righteousness on earth, for in these I delight," declares the LORD.
> —JEREMIAH 9:24

> Love is kind.
> —1 CORINTHIANS 13:4

PAUSE AND ADORE HIM.

CONFESSION

> Do you show contempt for the riches of his kindness, forbearance and patience, not realizing that God's kindness is intended to lead you to repentance?
> —ROMANS 2:4

> Consider therefore the kindness and sternness of God: sternness to those who fell, but kindness to you, provided that you continue in his kindness. Otherwise, you also will be cut off.
> —ROMANS 11:22

PAUSE AND CONFESS YOUR SINS.

Thanksgiving

"In a surge of anger I hid my face from you for a moment, but with everlasting kindness I will have compassion on you," says the Lord your Redeemer.
—Isaiah 54:8

I have loved you with an everlasting love; I have drawn you with unfailing love.
—Jeremiah 31:3

You gave me life and showed me kindness, and in your providence watched over my spirit.
—Job 10:12

I led them with cords of human kindness, with ties of love: I lifted the yoke from their neck and bent down to feed them.
—Hosea 11:4

Pause and thank him.

Supplication

Kind and gracious Lord, help _____ to "be kind and compassionate to others, forgiving others, just as in Christ God forgave him/her" (Ephesians 4:32).

Daily, may _____ "clothe himself/herself with compassion, kindness, humility, gentleness and patience" (Colossians 3:12).

"May the Lord show _____ kindness, as he/she shows kindness to others" (Ruth 1:8).

Pray for those who need to know the kindness of Christ.

REFLECTION

> *The first thing a kindness deserves is acceptance, the second, transmission.*
> —George MacDonald (1824–1905)

An image of kindness is portrayed in the film *Pay It Forward*. In the movie, a social studies teacher gives his class an assignment to think of an idea to change the world for the better. Embracing the task, one of his junior high students creates a plan to pass on kindnesses rather than pay them back. His actions set into motion a plethora of good deeds that impacted many far and wide.

There is One who performed the greatest act of kindness ever, whose actions have impacted the entire world. That was the kindness of God. The Hebrew word for God's kindness is *hesed*—his lovingkindness, his unfailing love, his mercy, his devotion, and his patience. God's *hesed* is displayed most vividly in his holding back judgment to give people time to repent. The apostle Paul said, "*God's kindness is meant to lead to repentance.*"[1]

Rephrasing George MacDonald, the first thing God's kindness deserves is acceptance; and the second, transmission. As a sinner, has God's kindness lead to your repentance? If not, ask God to forgive your sins and be your Savior. If God's kindness has already lead to your repentance, then "pay it forward." Spread the good news that out of lovingkindness God sent his Son as an atoning sacrifice for sins so sinners may be saved.

---

[1] ROMANS 2:4.

CHAPTER 32

GOODNESS

ADORATION

Praise God for his *goodness*!

> I will exalt you, my God the King;
>   I will praise your name for ever and ever.
> Every day I will praise you
>   and extol your name for ever and ever.
> Great is the LORD and most worthy of praise;
>   his greatness no one can fathom.
> One generation commends your works to another;
>   they tell of your mighty acts.
> They speak of the glorious splendor of your majesty—
>   and I will meditate on your wonderful works.
> They tell of the power of your awesome works—
>   and I will proclaim your great deeds.
> They celebrate your abundant goodness
>   and joyfully sing of your righteousness.
> —PSALM 145:1–7

And the LORD said, "I will cause all my goodness to pass in front of you, and I will proclaim my name, the LORD, in your presence."
—EXODUS 33:19

PAUSE AND ADORE HIM.

CONFESSION

Answer me, O LORD out of the goodness of your love; in your great mercy turn to me.
—PSALM 69:16

For I desire to "rid myself of all the offenses I have committed and get a new heart and a new spirit" (EZEKIEL 18:31).

PAUSE AND CONFESS YOUR SINS.

THANKSGIVING

His divine power has given us everything we need for a godly life through our knowledge of him who called us by his own glory and goodness.
—2 PETER 1:3

PAUSE AND THANK HIM.

SUPPLICATION

Good and gracious God, I pray that _____ will "make every effort to add to his/her faith goodness; and to goodness knowledge... so that he/she will be kept from being ineffective and unproductive in his/her knowledge of our Lord Jesus Christ" (2 PETER 1:5–8).

May "goodness and steadfast love follow _____ all the days of his/her life, and he/she will dwell in the house of the LORD forever" (PSALM 23:6).

PRAY FOR THOSE WHO NEED TO KNOW THE GOODNESS OF CHRIST.

REFLECTION

The attributes of God are those peculiarities which mark or define the mode of his existence, or which constitute his character.
—James Petigru Boyce, Abstract of Systematic Theology, 1887.

In systematic theology, the attributes of God are most commonly classified as either incommunicable or communicable. In his book, SYSTEMATIC THEOLOGY , Wayne Grudem defines the incommunicable attributes of God as "those attributes that God does not share or 'communicate' to others", and the communicable attributes as "those God shares or 'communicates' with us." An example of one of God's incommunicable attributes is holiness, which means set apart from sin, which man is not. Goodness is one of God's communicable attributes that he shares in part with his image-bearers.[1]

Goodness is part of God's essence. The Bible declares God is good and what he does is good.[2] "The goodness of God means that God is the final standard of good, and that all that God is and does is worthy of approval."[3] Therefore, there is nothing evil about God[4] and everything God does is ultimately for our good; his goodness leads to repentance.[5]

Juxtaposed to God's goodness is man's sinfulness. Because of the fall of man,[6] "every inclination of his heart is evil from childhood."[7] But in God's goodness he sent Jesus, who "purchased for God persons from every tribe and language and people and nation."[8]

Sinners who have been purchased for God with the blood of Christ are indwelt with the Holy Spirit. The Holy Spirit imparts the fruit of goodness to followers of Christ, enabling to them to be good and to do good, though not perfectly. Nevertheless, Christ's followers are to strive to emulate God's goodness.

---

[1] Wayne Grudem, SYSTEMATIC THEOLOGY, AN INTRODUCTION TO BIBLICAL DOCTRINE, (Zondervan 1994), 156.

[2] PSALM 119:68.

[3] Wayne Grudem, SYSTEMATIC THEOLOGY, AN INTRODUCTION TO BIBLICAL DOCTRINE, (Zondervan 1994), 197.

[4] HABAKKUK 1:13.

[5] ROMANS 2:4 NKJV.

[6] GENESIS 3.

[7] GENESIS 8:21.

[8] REVELATION 5:9.

"Our Christianity is a name, a shadow, unless, we resemble Him who, being the incarnate God, was incarnate goodness."[9] Therefore, as members of Christ's family, we are to embody God's goodness and, strive to, "Do all the good you can, by all the means you can, in all the ways you can, in all the places you can, at all the times you can, to all the people you can, as long as ever you can."[10]

---

[9] Attributed to John H. Aughey (1828–1911).

[10] Attributed to John Wesley, 1799, SERMONS ON SEVERAL OCCASIONS (A NEW EDITION) by the Rev. John Wesley (Late Fellow of Lincoln College, Oxford), Sermon 36, "The Law Established through Faith: Discourse 2." Printed by Edward Baines; Sold by T. Hannam, The Preachers in the New Itinerancy, and the Booksellers, Leeds, England, 486.

CHAPTER 33

FAITHFULNESS

ADORATION

Praise God! He is *faithful*!

> O LORD, you are my God; I will exalt you and praise your name, for in perfect faithfulness you have done marvelous things, things planned long ago.
> —ISAIAH 25:1

> Know therefore that the LORD your God is God; he is the faithful God, keeping his covenant of love to a thousand generations of those who love him and keep his commandments.
> —DEUTERONOMY 7:9

> I will sing of the LORD's great love forever; with my mouth I will make your faithfulness known through all generations.
> —PSALM 89:1

> O LORD God Almighty, who is like you? You are mighty, O LORD, and your faithfulness surrounds you.
> —PSALM 89:8

> All the ways of the LORD are loving and faithful toward those who keep the demands of his covenant.
> —PSALM 25:10

> For the word of the LORD is right and true; he is faithful in all he does.
> —PSALM 33:4

> Not to us, O LORD, not to us but to your name be the glory, because of your love and faithfulness.
> —PSALM 115:1

PAUSE AND ADORE HIM.

Confession

Father God, I have been faithless to you. Please "O Lord, hear my prayer, listen to my cry for mercy; in your faithfulness and righteousness come to my relief" (Psalm 143:1).

Pause and confess your sins.

Thanksgiving

Thanks be to God that "we have one who speaks to the Father in our defense—Jesus Christ, the Righteous One. He is the atoning sacrifice for our sins, and not only for ours but also for the sins of the whole world. Our sins have been forgiven on account of His name" (1 John 2:1–2, 12).

Through love and faithfulness sin is atoned for; through the fear of the Lord a man avoids evil.
—Proverbs 16:6

Pause and thank him.

Supplication

Faithful Father, I pray for _____ "to walk before you faithfully and with wholehearted devotion and to do what is good in your eyes" (2 Kings 20:3).

May _____ "use whatever gift he/she has received to serve others, as a faithful steward of God's grace" so that one day _____ may hear you say, "Well done, good and faithful servant!" (1 Peter 4:10; Matthew 25:21).

Pray for those who need to know the faithfulness of Christ.

REFLECTION

I have had the triple blessing of having a sister who is a faithful friend, my prayer partner, and my sister in Christ. Together, we have shared much. What we have shared most intimately are prayer requests. These request are mainly for family members and friends, along with those whom the Lord places upon our heart and across our path.

Often my sister asks, "How can I pray for you?" My most frequent response is, "Please pray that I may be found faithful." This prayer request became mine after hearing Steve Green's song, "Find Us Faithful."

I first heard Steve's song in 1998 when I was in the car with my dad. The two of us had been at the hospital visiting my dying mom. As I listened to the words, I thought not only of my precious mother, but also of those who had come before her, like her parents and grandparents, who had been faithful to the Lord. My heart was filled with gratitude for the spiritual inheritance I had received. My heart was also convicted that I, like them, was to leave a heritage of faith passed on through a godly life. At that moment, "Find Us Faithful" became my prayer and remains my prayer to this day.

FIND US FAITHFUL

We're pilgrims on the journey
Of the narrow road
And those who've gone before us line the way
Cheering on the faithful, encouraging the weary
Their lives a stirring testament to God's sustaining grace

Surrounded by so great a cloud of witnesses
Let us run the race not only for the prize
But as those who've gone before us
Let us leave to those behind us
The heritage of faithfulness
Passed on through godly lives

Oh may all who come behind us find us faithful
May the fire of our devotion light their way
May the footprints that we leave
Lead them to believe
And the lives we live inspire them to obey
Oh may all who come behind us find us faithful

After all our hopes and dreams have come and gone
And our children sift through all we've left behind
May the clues that they discover
And the memories they uncover
Become the light that leads them
To the road we each must find

Oh may all who come behind us find us faithful
Oh may all who come behind us find us faithful

—Steve Green, "FIND US FAITHFUL," Sparrow Records, 1988.

CHAPTER 34

GENTLENESS

ADORATION

Praise God! He is *gentle*.

> Praise the LORD, all you nations: extol him, all you peoples. For great is his love toward us, and the faithfulness of the LORD endures forever. Praise the LORD.
> —PSALM 117:1–2

> Praise be to the LORD, for he showed his wonderful love to me.
> —PSALM 31:21

> Remember, O LORD, your great mercy and love; for they are of old.
> —PSALM 25:6

Praise God for "the humility and gentleness of Christ" (2 CORINTHIANS 10:1).

Praise God, the Father of our Lord Jesus Christ, who said, "I am gentle and humble" (MATTHEW 11:29).

PAUSE AND ADORE HIM.

CONFESSION

> Who can discern his error? Forgive my hidden faults.
> —PSALM 19:12

> We have sinned, even as our fathers did; we have done wrong and acted wickedly.
> —PSALM 106:6

Consider therefore the kindness and sternness of God: sternness to those who fell, but kindness to you, provided that you continue in his kindness.
—ROMANS 11:22

PAUSE AND CONFESS YOUR SINS.

THANKSGIVING

May your unfailing love be for my comfort, according to your promise to your servant.
—PSALM 119:76

PAUSE AND THANK HIM.

SUPPLICATION

Heavenly Father, "remind _____ to be obedient, to be ready to do whatever is good, to slander no one, to be peaceable and considerate, and always to be gentle toward everyone" (TITUS 3:1–2).

May _____ 's "gentleness be evident to all" as he/she "bears with others in love" (PHILIPPIANS 4:5, EPHESIANS 4:2).

PRAY FOR THOSE WHO NEED TO KNOW THE GENTLENESS OF CHRIST.

REFLECTION

> *Both gentleness and meekness are born of power, not*
> *weakness. There is a pseudo-gentleness that is effeminate,*
> *and there is a pseudo-meekness that is cowardly. But a*
> *Christian is to be gentle and meek because those are God-*
> *like virtues. We should never be afraid, therefore, that*
> *gentleness of spirit means weakness of character. It takes*
> *strength, God's strength, to be truly gentle.[1]*
> —Jerry Bridges, THE PRACTICE OF GODLINESS.

My mother had a profound impact on everyone she met. From the greatest to the least, she made everyone feel special and valued because they were God's image-bearer. Etched in stone marking her grave are these words, *"She loved and she was loved. Her life was full of joy and grace. She enriched the lives of all who knew her."* Also inscribed in the stone is her favorite verse, PSALM 118:24, "This is the day the LORD has made; let us rejoice and be glad in it." My mother personifed this verse in the way she embraced each day with joy and gladness.

The epitome of love and kindness, this genteel lady was filled with God's grace and Southern charm. With the gift of hospitality, she opened her heart and home and welcomed all with ease. Through gentleness born in Christ, she exemplified courage and faith. Penned prior to her death, my husband's letter to my mother gives testimony to the impact gentleness and grace can have upon another.

---

[1] Jerry Bridges, THE PRACTICE OF GODLINESS, (NavPress, 1996), 181–182.

August 13, 1998

Dear Nell,

It is often easier to express myself in writing more thoroughly and succinctly than in person, so I am writing this letter even though I plan to see you this weekend...

... I want you to know how much you have taught me. From you I have learned there are depths to compassion, grace, giving and love that I never would have fathomed were it not for observing you live these virtues daily...

... It goes without saying that I appreciate your commitment to virtue and morality, but I am contemplating something deeper here...

Early in my life I made the mistake of thinking that some of the virtues you possess in such abundance were coupled inextricably with an absence of a fighting and tenacious spirit. Before I knew you, the people in my life who were fighters and exemplars of courage were always rough and tumble, street fighters who never surrender, such as my father and Gunner Ohlandt. Somehow, I had learned to assign courage and strength only to those who fought intensely and unswervingly in the field of athletics, business or politics. I had grown to consider only those who conquer with zeal, often with disregard for the virtues you possess so abundantly, as strong and courageous. I made the mistake of confusing grace and compassion as weakness. However, I stand corrected by your life and example...

Although your body is now very frail, in you there is great strength and character that cancer cannot destroy ... Disease has ravaged your body, but it has sharpened your spirit, producing a great example for us to follow. I will teach my boys to emulate their Nana in the face of adversity, for there is no better exemplar I know...

With deepest love and respect, I am your admiring son-in-law,

Chip

My husband's letter is evidence of the impact gentleness born of God's strength[2] can have upon another. Consider the impact your life can have for Christ as you live out your Christian faith and show gentleness to others.

---

[2] Jerry Bridges, THE PRACTICE OF GODLINESS, (NavPress, 1996), 181–182.

CHAPTER 35

SELF-CONTROL

ADORATION

I love you, O LORD, my strength. The LORD is my rock, my fortress and my deliverer; my God is my rock, in whom I take refuge. He is my shield and the horn of my salvation, my stronghold.
—PSALM 18:1–2

As for God, his way is perfect; the word of the LORD is flawless. He is a shield for all who take refuge in him. For who is God beside the LORD? And who is the Rock except our God?
—PSALM 18:30–31

You give me your shield of victory, and your right hand sustains me.
—PSALM 18:35

It is God who arms me with strength and makes my way perfect.
—PSALM 18:32

The LORD lives! Praise be to my Rock! Exalted be God my Savior! He is the God who avenges me.
—PSALM 18:46–47

PAUSE AND ADORE HIM.

CONFESSION

But mark this: There will be terrible times in the last days. People will be lovers of themselves, lovers of money, boastful, proud, abusive, disobedient to their parents, ungrateful, unholy, without love, unforgiving, slanderous, without self-control, brutal, not lovers of good, treacherous, rash, conceited, lovers of pleasure rather than lovers of God—having a form of godliness but denying its power. Have nothing to do with them.
—2 TIMOTHY 3:1–5

PAUSE AND CONFESS YOUR SINS.

THANKSGIVING

Yet he was merciful; he forgave their iniquities and did not destroy them. Time after time he restrained his anger and did not stir up his full wrath.
—PSALM 78:38

For the grace of God that brings salvation has appeared to all men. It teaches us to say "No" to ungodliness and worldly passions, and to live self-controlled, upright and godly lives in this present age, while we wait for the blessed hope—the glorious appearing of our great God and Savior, Jesus Christ, who gave himself for us to redeem us from all wickedness and to purify for himself a people that are his very own, eager to do what is good.
—TITUS 2:11–14

PAUSE AND THANK HIM.

SUPPLICATION

God is faithful. He will not let you be tempted beyond what you can bear. But when tempted, he will provide a way out.
—1 CORINTHIANS 10:13

God of all mercy and grace, I pray by the power of your Holy Spirit _____ will "say 'No' to ungodliness and worldly passions, and live a self-controlled, upright and godly life in this present age" (TITUS 2:12).

PRAY FOR THOSE WHO NEED SELF-CONTROL.

REFLECTION

THINK about this. The last, but surely not least, of the nine fruits of the Spirit is self-control.[1] Self-control can be described as temperance or moderation. It is restraint, particularly in regard to controlling one's passions and behavior. Given by God, self-control is empowered by the Holy Spirit's working in our lives to give the strength needed to say no to fleshly lust and desires. Though it sounds constricting, it is actually the virtue that gives freedom—freedom to enjoy the fullness of Christ's love and to live, as we were meant, full of his Spirit.

Now, THINK about this. "Where the mind goes, the body follows." It starts in the mind. Sexual immorality, alcohol abuse, drug addiction, pornography, coarse speech, gossip, and slander, all start in the mind.

THINK about it. Thoughtful desires give way to temptation; temptation gives way to sin.[2]

THINK about it. "Where the mind goes, the mouth follows." It starts in the mind and comes out of the mouth. With me, my thoughts give way to my tongue—my harsh, judgmental, boasting, divisive, complaining, manipulative, critical, argumentative, meddling, belittling, lying, cursing, slandering, gossiping, tactless tongue. In my case, unrestrained thoughts become hurtful, sinful words.

THINK about it. If sin begins in the mind, then "thought life is our first line of defense in the battle of self-control."[3] The Bible tells us to "say 'No' to ungodliness and worldly passions and to live self-controlled, upright and godly lives in this present age."[4]

---

[1] GALATIANS 5:22–23.

[2] JAMES 1:13–15.

[3] Jerry Bridges, THE PRACTICE OF GODLINESS, (NavPress, 1996), 138.

[4] TITUS 2:12.

THINK about it. God's Word and prayer are our defense. There-fore, "Set your heart and minds on things above"[5] and avoid falling into temptation and sin. With heart and mind set on things above, the Spirit of God will watch over, guard, protect, and give strength to withstand the "sinful desires which war with your soul."[6]

I need help with the conventional wisdom to think before I speak. Therefore, I came up with the following acronym for THINK. Now, before speaking I ask, "Is what I am about to say…"

True • Honoring to God • Inspirational • Necessary • Kind[7]

THINK of areas in which you need self-control. Ask yourself what you can do to keep tainted desires from giving way to temp-tations and turning into sin. Scripture implores, "Be self-controlled and alert. Your enemy the devil prowls around like a roaring lion looking for someone to devour. Resist him, standing firm in the faith."[8]

Christian, stand firm by looking to the Lord for strength. Ask for the Holy Spirit's help to say no to the worldly desires and pray for God to grant you self-control.

Finally, be strong in the LORD and in his mighty power. Put on the full armor of God so that you can take your stand against the devil's schemes… Stand firm!
—EPHESIANS 6:10–11, 14

---

[5] COLOSSIANS 3:1–4.

[6] 1 PETER 2:11.

[7] TRUE (ZECHARIAH 8:16, PROVERBS 12:17–19, 22); HONORING TO GOD (PSALM 19:14, COLOSSIANS 3:17); INSPIRATIONAL (1 THESSALONIANS 5:11; EPHESIANS 4:29); NECESSARY (PROVERBS 12:23, DEUTERONOMY 32:45–47); KIND (PROVERBS 16:24, TITUS 3:2)

[8] 1 PETER 5:8–9.

SECTION III

PRAYERS FOR PARTICULAR PEOPLE

CHAPTER 36

FAMILY AND FRIENDS

ADORATION

I will sing of the LORD's great love forever; with my mouth I will make your faithfulness known through all generations. I will declare that your love stands firm forever, that you have established your faithfulness in heaven itself.

You said, "I have made a covenant with my chosen one, I have sworn to David my servant, I will establish your line forever and make your throne firm through all generations." *Selah*

The heavens praise your wonders, O LORD, your faithfulness too, in the assembly of the holy ones. For who in the skies above can compare with the LORD? Who is like the LORD among the heavenly beings? In the council of the holy ones God is greatly feared; he is more awesome than all who surround him. O LORD God Almighty, who is like you? You are mighty, O LORD, and your faithfulness surrounds you.

You rule over the surging sea; when its waves mount up, you still them. You crushed Rahab like one of the slain; with your strong arm you scattered your enemies. The heavens are yours, and yours also the earth; you founded the world and all that is in it. You created the north and the south; Tabor and Hermon sing for joy at your name. Your arm is endowed with power; your hand is strong, your right hand exalted.

Righteousness and justice are the foundation of your throne; love and faithfulness go before you. Blessed are those who have learned to acclaim you, who walk in the light of your presence, O LORD. They rejoice in your name all day long; they exult in your righteousness. For you are their glory and strength, and by your favor you exalt our horn. Indeed, our shield belongs to the LORD, our king to the Holy One of Israel.
—PSALM 89:1–18

PAUSE AND ADORE HIM.

CONFESSION

"I will judge you, each according to his ways," declares the Sovereign, LORD. "Repent! Turn away from all your offenses; then sin will not be your downfall. Rid yourselves of all the offenses you have committed and get a new heart and a new spirit. For I take no pleasure in the death of anyone," declares the Sovereign LORD. "Repent and live!"
—EZEKIEL 18:30–32

PAUSE AND CONFESS YOUR SINS.

THANKSGIVING

For Christ died for sins once for all, the righteous for the unrighteous, to bring you to God. He was put to death in the body but made alive by the Spirit.
—1 PETER 3:18

Praise be to the God and Father of our Lord Jesus Christ! In his great mercy he has given us new birth into a living hope through the resurrection of Jesus Christ from the dead, and into an inheritance that can never perish, spoil or fade—kept in heaven for you.
—1 PETER 1:3–4

PAUSE AND THANK HIM.

SUPPLICATION

Jesus said, "You are my friends if you do what I command." Your command is, "Love each other" (JOHN 15:14, 17).

Abba Father, help _____ to love others (JOHN 15:17).

Holy Spirit, empower _____ to "live in harmony with others; be sympathetic, love as brothers, be compassionate and humble. May _____ not repay evil with evil or insult with insult, but with blessing, because to this _____ was called, so that he/she may inherit a blessing" (1 PETER 3:8–9).

If _____ "desires to love life and see good days, he/she must keep his/her tongue from evil and his/her lips from speaking deceit. Help _____ turn away from evil and do good; let him/her seek peace and pursue it. For the eyes of the Lord are on the righteous, and his ears are open to their prayers. But the face of the Lord is against those who do evil" (1 PETER 3:10–12 ESV).

PRAY FOR FRIENDS AND FAMILY.

REFLECTION

Proud to carry her husband's surname, my paternal grandmother would tell her children as they left home, "Remember your name is Laffitte." To her, the name embodied good character and implied their children were to conduct themselves with love, integrity, dignity, and respect. She did not want them to tarnish the reputation they had inherited from their father. Like Solomon, she believed, "a good name is better than fine perfume."[1]

Like my grandmother's children, everyone has been given or inherited a name. Some convey dignity and respect, others shame. How much importance should we put in our earthly names?

Recently my pastor posed a provocative exercise regarding our familial names. He asked the congregants, "In the next few seconds, can you tell the person sitting beside you the maiden name of your maternal great-grandmother—that is the grandmother of your mother?" After a brief congregational buzz, many could not answer. He, too, confessed he called his mom to ask. The call came with a

---

[1] ECCLESIASTES 7:1.

pause, then she answered, "It was 'Mac-something.' She died young and I really don't remember." Sad, but true, most of our names will not be remembered in a few generations, not even by our family.

However, there is a family name that is eternal. Abba Father, the one who is the "name above all names," gives those who trust in his Son as savior a new name. Jesus says, "I will give him a white stone with a new name written on it, known only to him who receives it… I will write on him the name of my God and the name of the city of my God, the new Jerusalem, which is coming down out of heaven from my God; and I will also write on him my new name."[2]

Follower of Christ, your new name carries weight and glory. As an adopted* son or daughter of the Most High King, your reputation is now linked to his. You are his name-bearer. Therefore, "remember your name" and live with biblical love, integrity, dignity, and respect in such a way to bring God all of the glory, honor, and praise due his Most Holy Name.

* "Adoption is an act of God whereby he makes us members of his family."[3] The Bible says, "God sent forth his Son, to redeem those under the law, that we might receive adoption as sons."[4] Upon adoption, "The Spirit himself testifies with our spirit that we are God's children…then heirs."[5] When adopted, we are given a new name,[6] which signifies a renewed relationship and new character.

---

[2] REVELATION 2:17; 3:12B.

[3] Wayne Grudem, SYSTEMATIC THEOLOGY: AN INTRODUCTION TO BIBLICAL DOCTRINE, (Zondervan 1994), 736.

[4] GALATIANS 4:5, ESV.

[5] ROMANS 8:15–17.

[6] REVELATION 2:17; ISAIAH 56:5, 62:2, 65:15.

CHAPTER 37

MISSIONARIES AND MINISTRIES

Be not ashamed of the gospel. Go and make disciples!

ADORATION

Shout with joy to God, all the earth! Sing the glory of his name; make his praise glorious! Say to God, "How awesome are your deeds! So great is your power that your enemies cringe before you. All the earth bows down to you: they sing praise to you, they sing praise to your name."
—PSALM 66:1–4

PAUSE AND ADORE HIM!

CONFESSION

The wrath of God is being revealed from heaven against all the godlessness and wickedness of men who suppress the truth by their wickedness.
—ROMANS 1:18

For although they knew God, they neither glorified him as God nor gave thanks to him.
—ROMANS 1:21

Therefore, God gave them over in the sinful desires of their hearts to sexual impurity for the degrading of their bodies with one another.
—ROMANS 1:24

God gave them over to shameful lusts. They have become filled with every kind of wickedness, evil, greed and depravity. They are full of envy, murder, strife, deceit and malice. They are gossips, slanderers, God-haters, insolent, arrogant and boastful; they invent ways of doing evil; they disobey their parents; they are senseless, faithless, heartless, ruthless. Although they know

God's righteous decree that those who do such things deserve death, they not only continue to do these very things but also approve of those who practice them.
—ROMANS 1:28–32

PAUSE AND CONFESS YOUR SINS.

THANKSGIVING

Therefore, there is no condemnation for those who are in Christ Jesus, because through Christ Jesus the law of the Spirit of life set me free from the law of sin and death. For what the law was powerless to do in that it was weakened by the sinful nature, God did by sending his own Son in the likeness of sinful man to be a sin offering.
—ROMANS 8:1–3

PAUSE AND THANK HIM.

SUPPLICATION

Father in heaven, I pray you will "set _____ apart for the gospel of God" (ROMANS 1:1).

May _____ "not be ashamed of the gospel," but know it is "the power of God for the salvation of everyone who believes" (ROMANS 1:16).

Give _____ the desire to "spread this good news and therefore go and make disciples of men" (MATTHEW 28:19).

May _____ "be a fisher of men" (MATTHEW 4:19).

PRAY FOR MINISTERS, MINISTRIES, AND MISSIONARIES.

REFLECTION

Shortly before Jesus Christ ascended into heaven, he spoke to his disciples the words known as *The Great Commission*. Recorded in MATTHEW 28:18–20, Jesus articulated what he expected his disciples and followers to do in his absence. His imperatives were—*go, make, baptize, teach, obey*. The primary focus of his command was to *make* disciples. *Go, baptize, teach*, and *obey* were given as the means to fulfill this command.

Many people have focused primarily on the word *go*, erroneously thinking it means to pull up your tent pegs and head to a distant land. This calling is definitely for some. Yet, the word *go* in the verse is actually a participle meaning "as you are going". Therefore, as you go about your day, make disciples.

Fellow believer, you are called to be a "fisher of men."[1] Wherever the Lord places you, he wants you to evangelize. Make disciples of those you encounter. Teach them the truths of the gospel. Charge them to obey the Lord's commands. Encourage them to be baptized as an outward sign of their inward commitment to follow Christ. In doing these things, you will be fulfilling the Great Commission.

> *You will receive power when the Holy Spirit comes on you;*
> *and you will be my witnesses in Jerusalem and in all Judea*
> *and Samaria, and to the ends of the earth.*
> —ACTS 1:8

---

[1] MATTHEW 4:19.

CHAPTER 38

AUTHORITY

ADORATION

Jesus came to them and said, "All authority in heaven and on earth has been given to me."
—MATTHEW 28:18

Acknowledge and take to heart this day that the LORD is God in heaven above and on the earth below. There is no other.
—DEUTERONOMY 4:39

For the LORD your God is a consuming fire, a jealous God.
—DEUTERONOMY 4:24

For the LORD your God, who is among you, is a great and awesome God.
—DEUTERONOMY 7:21

PAUSE AND ADORE HIM.

CONFESSION

Lord, we are a stiff-necked people indeed! We have sinned against you; we have made many idols and been quick to turn aside from the way that You have commanded us. We have grown cold and callous to You and Your Word. Please overlook our stubbornness, wickedness and sin. We ask for your forgiveness. (DEUTERONOMY 9:13, 16, 18; 9:26–29)

But I want you to know that the Son of Man has authority on earth to forgive sins.
—MATTHEW 9:6

PAUSE AND CONFESS YOUR SINS.

THANKSGIVING

To him who is able to keep you from falling and to present you
before his glorious presence without fault and with great joy—to
the only God our Savior be glory, majesty, power and authority, through Jesus Christ our Lord, before all ages, now and
forevermore.
—JUDE 24–25

For with the LORD is unfailing love and with him is full redemption. He himself will redeem us from our sins.
—PSALM 130:7–8

PAUSE AND THANK HIM.

SUPPLICATION

I urge, then, first of all, that requests, prayers, intercessions and
thanksgiving be made for everyone—for kings and all those in
authority, that we may live peaceful and quiet lives in all godliness and holiness. This is good, and pleases God our Savior,
who wants all men to be saved and to come to a knowledge of
the truth. For there is one God and one mediator between God
and men, the man Christ Jesus, who gave himself as a ransom
for all men."
—1 TIMOTHY 2:1–6

Supreme Ruler, may _____ be "subject to the governing
authorities and know there is no authority except from God, and
those that exist have been instituted by God" (ROMANS 13:1).

Therefore, help _____ "submit for the Lord's sake to
every authority instituted among men; whether to the king, as
the supreme authority, or to governors" (1 PETER 2:13).

By the power of your Holy Spirit help _____ "show proper respect to everyone: Love the brotherhood of believers, fear God, honor the king" (1 PETER 2:17).

PRAY FOR THOSE IN AUTHORITY: CHURCH, HOME, BUSINESS, GOVERNMENT, SCHOOL.

REFLECTION

> *If men were angels, no government would be necessary. If angels were to govern men, neither external nor internal controls on government would be necessary. In framing a government which is to be administered by men over men, the great difficulty lies in this: you must first enable the government to control the governed; and the next place, oblige it to control itself.*
> —James Madison, FEDERALIST PAPER NO. 51 (1788)

In constructing the United States Constitution, the framers employed a Judeo-Christian view of human nature. They understood men were made in God's image and, therefore, capable of great good; but they were also fallen and sinful, and therefore capable of great evil as well.

In light of this reality, beneficent political governance was possible, but the baser elements of human nature had to be constrained, both in government and in the governed. Unbridled, men seek to dominate and rule over other men; hence, a "check and balance" form of government was instituted so that man's lust for power would be harnessed, and mankind could be protected from oppressive government.

America's government, like all secular government, originated with God. Wayne Grudem writes regarding human government:

It was instituted in principle by God after the flood (see Gen. 9:6), and is clearly stated to be given by God in Romans 13:1: "There is no authority except from God, and those that exist have been instituted by God." It is clear that government is a gift from God for mankind generally, for Paul says the ruler is "God's servant for your good" and that he is "the servant of God to execute his wrath on the wrongdoer" (Romans 13:4).[1]

Ultimate authority, though, belongs to our omniscient, omnipotent, omnipresent God who is sovereign over all. His rule supersedes all other authority—whether it be governmental, spousal, parental, school or otherwise. God proclaimed this in his Word.[2]

Many Protestant churches acknowledge the authority of God and his Word in the doctrinal statement: "The Bible is our only rule for faith and practice." As the inspired, inerrant, infallible word of God,[3] it has absolute authority in the life of the believer and equips them for service. A. A. Hodge wrote, "Whatever God teaches or commands is of sovereign authority ... The Scripture of the Old and New Testaments are the only organs through which, during the present dispensation, God conveys to us a knowledge of his will about what we are to believe concerning himself, and what duties he requires of us."[4]

When we profess, "The Bible is our only rule for faith and practice," we are declaring we hold God's Holy Word to be the ultimate guide for what we believe and what we do. Because his Word supersedes all other authority, we can cry with the Reformers, *Sola Scriptura.*

---

[1] Wayne Grudem, Systematic Theology: An Introduction to Biblical Doctrine, (Zondervan 1994), 661.

[2] Romans 13:1.

[3] 2 Timothy 3:16–17.

[4] A. A. Hodge, Outlines of Theology, Ch. 5.

Note: During the Protestant Reformation, five Latin phrases became the hallmark battle cry of the Reformers. They used these phrases to distinguished their beliefs from the teachings of the established Roman Catholic Church. They are:

> *Sola Scriptura*: Scripture alone
> *Sola Fide*: faith alone
> *Sola Gratia*: grace alone
> *Solus Christus*: Christ alone
> *Soli Deo Gloria*: to the glory of God alone

For further study on the authority of Scripture read:
2 TIMOTHY 3:16–17; 2 PETER 1:21; and ACTS 1:16.

CHAPTER 39

WEAK AND SICK

Is any one of you in trouble? He should pray. Is anyone happy? Let him sing songs of praise. Is any one of you sick? He should call the elders of the church to pray over him and anoint him with oil in the name of the Lord. And the prayer offered in faith will make the sick person well; the Lord will raise him up. If he has sinned, he will be forgiven. Therefore, confess your sins to each other and pray for each other so that you may be healed. The prayer of a righteous man is powerful and effective.
—James 5:13–16

ADORATION

Praise be to God, our *Great Physician*, for his grace and power!

Praise the LORD, O my soul; all my inmost being, praise his holy name. Praise the LORD, O my soul, and forget not all his benefits—who forgives all your sins and heals all your diseases, who redeems your life from the pit and crowns you with love and compassion, who satisfies your desires with good things so that your youth is renewed like the eagle's.
—PSALM 103:1–5

I am the LORD, who heals you.
—EXODUS 15:26

My grace is sufficient for you, for my power is made perfect in weakness. Therefore, I will boast all the more gladly about my weakness, so that Christ's power may rest on me.
—2 CORINTHIANS 12:9

PAUSE AND ADORE HIM.

CONFESSION

Jesus said to them, "It is not the healthy who need a doctor, but the sick. I have not come to call the righteous, but sinners."
—MATTHEW 9:12

Have mercy on me, LORD, heal me, for I have sinned against you.
—PSALM 41:4

Restore us again, God our Savior, and put away your displeasure toward us.
—PSALM 85:4

PAUSE AND CONFESS YOUR SINS.

THANKSGIVING

This is what the LORD said, "I will cleanse them from all the sin they have committed against me and will forgive all their sins of rebellion against me."
—JEREMIAH 33:8

LORD my God, I called to you for help, and you healed me.
—PSALM 30:2

Thanks be to God!

PAUSE AND THANK HIM.

SUPPLICATION

Great Physician, please bring healing to _____ .

"Have mercy on _____ , LORD, for _____ is faint; heal _____ , Lord, for his/her bones are in agony" (PSALM 6:2).

"Be merciful to _____, L<small>ORD</small>, for _____ is in distress; _____ 's eyes have grown weak with sorrow, his/ her soul and body with grief" (P<small>SALM</small> 31:9).

May _____ "enjoy good health and may all go well with him/her" (3 J<small>OHN</small> 2).

"The L<small>ORD</small> bless _____ and keep _____; the L<small>ORD</small> make his face shine upon _____ and be gracious to _____; the L<small>ORD</small> turn his face toward _____ and give _____ peace" (N<small>UMBERS</small> 6:24–26).

R<small>EFLECTION</small>

> *People make too much parade of their troubles and too much fuss about them; the fact is we are all born to tribulation, as we also are to innumerable joys, and there is no sense in being too much depressed or elated by either.*[1]
> —Elizabeth Prentiss

Why is there sickness? Why is there pain? Why are there trials and tribulations? We must literally go back to the beginning, to a Christian doctrine known as *Original Sin*. Its origin is the Garden of Eden, when Adam and Eve sinned. They "failed to conform to God's moral law not only in action and in attitude, but also in moral nature."[2] Since that time, Adam's sin and guilt has been transmitted to all mankind.[3] With sin came trials, tribulations, pain, suffering, and death. But why?

---

[1] A<small>TTRIBUTE TO</small> E<small>LIZABETH</small> P<small>RENTISS</small>, T<small>HE</small> L<small>IFE AND</small> L<small>ETTERS OF</small> E<small>LIZABETH</small> P<small>RENTISS</small>.

[2] Wayne Grudem, S<small>YSTEMATIC</small> T<small>HEOLOGY</small>, A<small>N</small> I<small>NTRODUCTION TO</small> B<small>IBLICAL</small> D<small>OCTRINE</small>, (Zondervan 1994), 490.

[3] G<small>ENESIS</small> 3.

First, we must understand that God has an ultimate purpose and a plan in all things, even our suffering. He says, "For I know the plans I have for you," declares the LORD, "plans to prosper you and not harm you, plans to give you hope and a future."[4] This verse does not mean we will be spared hardship here on earth, but that the future (eternity in heaven) is glorious for those who put their faith and trust in Jesus.

At times, it is difficult to understand God's means to the end, as his methods are often different than what we may hope, dream, or imagine. Scripture states, "My thoughts are not your thoughts, neither are your ways my ways," declares the LORD.[5] We tend to focus on problems rather than his purposes. Rarely do we ask, "What does God want to teach me in and through this sickness, this disease, this suffering? What good can come from it?" At times, we clinch our fist in anger and rebel rather than see the trial as part of our sanctification process.

Often trials and tribulations are the megaphone God uses to call people to himself. My precious mother would have agreed. Through her battle with cancer, she gave witness to God's goodness and thanked him for allowing her to experience that dreaded disease. She said, "The disease has been my blessing to endure," because it drew her closer to God in utter dependence and reliance upon him. She agreed with the psalmist, "It was good for me to be afflicted so that I might learn your decrees."[6] She learned through her sickness to trust God for all her needs.

My friend, don't waste pain and sufferings. Trust in God's purpose and plan. May trials cause you to draw near to God, in utter dependence upon him.

Praise be to the God and Father of our Lord Jesus Christ, the Father of compassion and the God of all comfort, who comforts us in all our troubles, so that we may comfort those in trouble with the comfort we ourselves have received from God.
—2 CORINTHIANS 1:3–4

---

[4] JEREMIAH 29:11.

[5] ISAIAH 55:9.

[6] PSALM 119:71.

CHAPTER 40

THE NEXT GENERATION

ADORATION

Know therefore that the LORD your God is God; he is the faithful God, keeping his covenant of love to a thousand generations of those who love him and keep his commandments.
—DEUTERONOMY 7:9

He established a testimony in Jacob and appointed a law in Israel, which he commanded our fathers to teach to their children, that the next generation might know them, the children yet unborn, and arise and tell them to their children so that they should set their hope in God and not forget the works of God.
—PSALM 78:5–7 ESV

I will sing of the LORD's great love forever; with my mouth I will make your faithfulness known through all generations. I will declare that your love stands firm forever, that you established your faithfulness in the heaven itself.
—PSALM 89:1–2

For the LORD is good and his love endures forever; his faithfulness continues through all generations.
—PSALM 100:5

He remembers his covenant forever, the promise he made, for a thousand generations.
—PSALM 105:8

But the plans of the LORD stand firm forever, the purposes of his heart through all generations.
—PSALM 33:11

We your people, the sheep of your pasture, will praise you forever; from generation to generation we will proclaim your praise.
—PSALM 79:13

PAUSE AND ADORE HIM.

CONFESSION

Your Word says, "I, the LORD your God, am a jealous God,
punishing the children for the sin of the fathers to the third and
fourth generation of those of hate me" (EXODUS 20:5).

Father God, we are "a stubborn and rebellious generation, a generation whose heart is not steadfast, whose spirit was not faithful
to God" (PSALM 78:8 ESV).

Do not hold against us the sins of past generations, may your
mercy come quickly to meet us, for we are in desperate need.
Help us, O God our Savior, for the glory of your name; deliver
us and forgive our sins for your name's sake.
—PSALM 79:8–9

Lord, forgive us, for we are "a crooked and depraved generation" (PHILIPPIANS 2:15).

PAUSE AND CONFESS YOUR SINS.

THANKSGIVING

We have an advocate with the Father, Jesus Christ the righteous.
He is the propitiation for our sins, and not for ours only but also
for the sins of the whole world... I am writing to you, dear children, because your sins are forgiven for his name's sake.
—1 JOHN 2:1–2; 12 ESV

I delight greatly in the LORD; my soul rejoices in my God. For he has clothed me with garments of salvation and arrayed me in a robe of righteousness.
—ISAIAH 61:10

PAUSE AND THANK HIM.

SUPPLICATION

God our Father, I pray _____ "will be called an oak of righteousness, a planting of the LORD for the display of his splendor. May _____ take part in rebuilding the ancient ruins and restoring the places long devastated. May your power be at work in _____ 's life so that _____ may be part of renewing the ruined cities that have been devastated for generations. May _____ be called a priest of the LORD, a minister of our God" (ISAIAH 61:3–4, 6).

REFLECTION

> *The greatest legacy one can pass on to one's children and grandchildren is not money or other material things accumulated in one's life, but rather a legacy of character and faith.*[1]
> —Billy Graham

The dirt road leading to my grandparent's house is lined with two hundred-year-old Live Oak trees. Each time I pull off the highway and go down the dusty drive underneath their broad branches, I marvel at their sheer majesty. Like their boughs, my heart lifts up in praise to my Creator. Their magnificence incites all sorts of emotions and prayers.

---

[1] Attributed to Billy Graham.

As I gaze upon the grandeur of the mighty oaks, my heart is filled with thanksgiving for eyes to see the beauty God has made. The trees and surrounding creation cause me to express prayers of gratitude. They also trigger prayers for the time to come in the woods with family and friends. They make me reflect on the years spent at the house with my grandparents and parents, who planted seeds of faith. They make me grateful for all the relatives and friends I have been able to enjoy life with under their canopy.

As the years have passed and the trees have grown, so have the numbers that have passed under their sturdy boughs. Now a fifth generation enjoys the home. Roots of faith planted by my grandparents still grow. And these trees continue to incite prayer in me, more fervently than ever.

My fervent prayers are for the next generation and generations yet to come. I pray they will be like Live Oak trees, sturdy and strong; that they remain verdant throughout the cold of winter; that they grow where planted; that they support other life and produce nourishing fruit. May the generations to come stand tall with arms lifted high in praise to the One who made them. May they be "like a tree planted by streams of water, which yeilds its fruit in season and whose leaf does not wither."[2] My earnest prayer for the generations to come is they "be called oaks of righteousness, a planting of the LORD for the display of His splendor."[3]

---

[2] PSALM 1:3.

[3] ISAIAH 61:3.

SECTION IV

PRAYERS BY TOPIC OR THEME

CHAPTER 41

Marks of a Christian

Adoration

How great you are, Sovereign Lord! There is no one like you, and there is no God but you.
—2 Samuel 7:22

May the peoples praise you, O God; may all the peoples praise you. May the nations be glad and sing for joy, for you rule the peoples justly and guide the nations of the earth. May the peoples praise you, O God; may all the peoples praise you.
—Psalm 67:3–5

Sovereign Lord, you are God! Your covenant is trustworthy, and you have promised these good things to your servant.
—2 Samuel 7:28

Lord, you are a compassionate and gracious God, slow to anger, abounding in love and faithfulness.
—Psalm 86:15

Who is like you, Lord God Almighty? You, Lord, are mighty, and your faithfulness surrounds you.
—Psalm 89:8

Praise the Lord, my soul.
—Psalm 104:1

Pause and adore him.

Confession

It is true! I have sinned against the Lord.
—Joshua 7:20

Search me, O God, and know my heart; test me and know my anxious thoughts. See if there is any offensive way in me, and lead me in the way everlasting.
—PSALM 139:23–24

PAUSE AND CONFESS YOUR SINS.

THANKSGIVING

Come and listen, all you who fear God; let me tell you what he has done for me. I cried out to him with my mouth; his praise was on my tongue. If I had cherished sin in my heart, the Lord would not have listened; but God has surely listened and heard my voice in prayer. Praise be to God, who has not rejected my prayer or withheld his love from me!
—PSALM 66:16–20

Praise be to the Lord, to God our Savior, who daily bears our burdens. Our God is a God who saves; from the Sovereign LORD comes escape from death.
—PSALM 68:19–20

PAUSE AND THANK HIM.

SUPPLICATION

Lord God, I pray _____ 's words and actions be marks of his/her love and commitment to you.

May _____ 's "love be sincere; help _____ hate what is evil and cling to what is good. By the power of your Holy Spirit may _____ be devoted to one another in brotherly love and honor others above himself/herself. May _____ be joyful in hope, patient in affliction, faithful in prayer" (Romans 12:9–13).

REFLECTION

As a teenager, young in my faith, I wore a large cross on a chain around my neck as an outward sign of the inward commitment I had made to follow Jesus. Even though it had no power in and of itself, the tangible cross gave me peace and comfort. At times I literally clung to my necklace as I reflected upon biblical truths like God is with me and will never leave me or forsake me.[1] Many people display outward symbols of Christian faith. But we must be vigilant to avoid the error of believing these symbols are a mark of true faith.

What is the distinguishing mark of a Christian? Shortly after Jesus and his disciples gathered for the Last Supper and Judas departed their company, Jesus addressed his disciples and shared with them the true mark of a Christian.

> *My children... A new command I give you: Love one another. As I have loved you, so you must love one another. By this all men will know that you are my disciples, if you love one another.*
> —JOHN 13:33–35

The command to love was not new. The Lord told Moses to tell the Israelites "not to seek revenge or bear a grudge, but love your neighbor as yourself."[2] Jesus' command was dramatic because his disciples were to follow his example of sacrificial love in order to bring unbelievers to faith in him.

If I am truthful, rarely do I love the way the Lord commands. It is much easier to put on a Christian symbol than it is to sacrificially love. I have asked myself, "How often do I sincerely love others with the intent of making disciples?" As a follower of Christ, that is what I am called to do. As his follower, you are too.

---

[1] DEUTERONOMY 31:6, 8; HEBREWS 13:5; JOSHUA 1.

[2] LEVITICUS 19:18.

Dear children, let us not love with words and tongue but with actions and in truth.
—1 JOHN 3:18

CHAPTER 42

ATTITUDE

ADORATION

Come, let us sing for joy to the LORD; let us shout aloud to the Rock of our salvation. Let us come before him with thanksgiving and extol him with music and song.

For the LORD is the great God, the great King above all gods. In his hand are the depths of the earth, and the mountain peaks belong to him. The sea is his, for he made it, and his hands formed the dry land.

Come, let us bow down in worship, let us kneel before the LORD our Maker; for he is our God and we are the people of his pasture, the flock under his care.
—PSALM 95:1–7

PAUSE AND ADORE HIM.

CONFESSION

At one time we too were foolish, disobedient, deceived and enslaved by all kinds of passions and pleasures. We lived in malice and envy, being hated and hating one another.
—TITUS 3:3

PAUSE AND CONFESS YOUR SINS.

THANKSGIVING

But when the kindness and love of God our Savoir appeared, he saved us, not because of righteous things we had done, but because of his mercy. He saved us through the washing of rebirth and renewal by the Holy Spirit, whom he poured out on us generously through Jesus Christ our Savior, so that, having been justified by his grace, we might become heirs having the hope of eternal life.
—TITUS 3:4–7

PAUSE AND THANK HIM.

SUPPLICATION

Heavenly Father, I pray, "Whatever happens, _____ will conduct himself/herself in a manner worthy of the gospel of Christ" (PHILIPPIANS 1:27).

May _____ 's "attitude be the same as that of Christ Jesus and his/her nature be that of a humble servant" (PHILIPPIANS 2:5–7).

By the power of your Holy Spirit, help _____ "put off his/her old self, which is being corrupted by its deceitful desires; to be made new in the attitude of his/her mind; and to put on the new self, created to be like God in true righteousness and holiness" (EPHESIANS 4:23–24).

I want to stress these things, so that those who have trusted in God may be careful to devote themselves to doing what is good. These things are excellent and profitable for everyone.
—TITUS 3:8

REFLECTION

> *The longer I live, the more I realize the impact of attitude on life. Attitude, to me, is more important than facts. It is more important than the past, than education, than money, than circumstances, than failures, than successes, than what other people think or say or do. It is more important than appearance, giftedness or skill. It will make or break a company ... a church ... a home. The remarkable thing is we have a choice every day regarding the attitude we will embrace for that day. We cannot change our past... we cannot change the fact that people will act in a certain way. We cannot change the inevitable. The only thing we can do is play on the one string we have, and that is our attitude...I am convinced that life is 10% what happens to me and 90% how I react to it. And so it is with you...we are in charge of our attitudes.[1]*
> —Charles R. Swindoll, THE GRACE AWAKENING

From the confines of a dark, musty cell, Paul writes a letter of joy. This letter is the book of Philippians. In four chapters he mentions sixteen times the concept of rejoicing or joy. Prisoner Paul could express joy because he knew the resurrection power of the Lord Jesus Christ. He "considered everything a loss compared to the surpassing greatness of knowing Christ Jesus as Lord."[2] Through faith and trust in the Lord, Paul had learned to be joyful and content whatever his circumstance.[3]

With an attitude of gratitude, Paul opens his letter expressing his thanksgiving for the believers and telling them of his prayers of joy

---

[1] Chuck Swindoll, THE GRACE AWAKENING, (Thomas Nelson, 2012).

[2] PHILIPPIANS 3:8–10.

[3] PHILIPPIANS 4:11–13.

for them because of their partnership in the gospel.[4] He continues his letter with words of exhortation and encouragement.

A salient point Paul makes in his letter is for believers to be Christ-like in their attitude. "Whatever happens, conduct yourselves in a manner worthy of the gospel of Christ."[5] He goes on to encourage believers to be like-minded; to do nothing out of selfish ambition or vain conceit; in humility to think of others better than themselves; to look not only after their interest but also the interest of others.[6] He said, "Your attitude should be the same as that of Christ Jesus," a humble servant who demonstrated humility and self-sacrificing service, one that imitated Christ's love and nature.[7]

God's will is that we be "made new in the attitudes of our minds; and put on the new self, created to be like God in true righteousness and holiness."[8] Our attitude changes as the Holy Spirit fills us, and as we spend time in God's Word and in prayer. God will transform our minds, so we can reflect Christ's attitude and experience the true joy, peace, and contentment Paul experienced, whatever our circumstance.

[4] PHILIPPIANS 1:4–5.

[5] PHILIPPIANS 1:27.

[6] PHILIPPIANS 2:2–4.

[7] EPHESIANS 5:1.

[8] EPHESIANS 4:23–24.

CHAPTER 43

OVERCOMING EVIL WITH GOOD

ADORATION

I will praise you forever for what you have done; in your name I will hope, for your name is good. I will praise you in the presence of your saints.
—PSALM 52:9

Good and upright is the LORD; therefore he instructs sinners in his ways.
—PSALM 25:8

I will sing to the LORD, for he has been good to me.
—PSALM 13:6

No one is good—except God alone.
—LUKE 18:19

Praise the LORD. Give thanks to the LORD, for he is good; his love endures forever.
—PSALM 106:1

PAUSE AND ADORE HIM.

CONFESSION

God hath appointed a day, wherein He will judge the world in righteousness by Jesus Christ, to whom all power and judgment is given of the Father. In which day... all persons that have lived upon earth shall appear before the tribunal of Christ, to give an account of their thoughts, words, and deeds; and to receive according to what they have done in the body, whether good or evil.
—Westminster Confession of FAITH 33:1

Remember not the sins of my youth and my rebellious ways; according to your love remember me, for you are good, O LORD.
—PSALM 25:7

The heart is deceitful above all things and beyond cure. Who can understand it? I, the LORD, search the heart and examine the mind, to reward each person according to their conduct, according to what their deeds deserve.
—JEREMIAH 17:9–10

PAUSE AND CONFESS YOUR SINS.

THANKSGIVING

We love because he first loved us.
—1 JOHN 4:19

May our Lord Jesus Christ himself and God our Father, who loved us and by his grace gave us eternal encouragement and good hope, encourage your hearts and strengthen you in every good deed and word.
—2 THESSALONIANS 2:16–17

PAUSE AND THANK HIM!

SUPPLICATION

Father God, I pray _____ will not repay anyone evil for evil.
May _____ be careful to do what is right in the eyes of everyone.
As far as it depends on _____, help _____ live at peace with everyone.
May _____ not take revenge but leave room for God's wrath, for it is written: "'It is mine to avenge; I will repay,' says the Lord."

On the contrary: If _____ 's enemy is hungry, may he/she feed him; if he is thirsty, may _____ give him something to drink. In doing this, _____ will heap burning coals on his head.

By the power of your Holy Spirit may _____ "not be overcome by evil but overcome evil with good" (ROMANS 12:17–21).

REFLECTION

> *This is a very pithy verse, and the form of it greatly assists the memory. It is worthy to be called a Christian proverb. I would recommend every Christian man to learn it by heart and have it ready for use; for there are a great many proverbs, which convey a very different sense, and these are often quoted to give the weight of authority to unchristian principles. Here is an inspired proverb: carry it with you and use it as a weapon with which to parry the thrusts of the world's wisdom. "Be not overcome of evil, but overcome evil with good."*
> —Charles H. Spurgeon. October 8, 1876. Sermon No.1317. METROPOLITAN TABERNACLE PULPIT, Volume 22.

The focus verse this week, "Do not be overcome by evil, but overcome evil with good," is taken from ROMANS 12, where Paul is writing to Christians about their responsibility to live and love sacrificially. He concludes the chapter with the exhortation to "overcome evil with good."[1]

As said in the quote above, Spurgeon felt Paul's admonition to be so valid that he encouraged every Christian to memorize ROMANS 12:21. Spurgeon knew "good," especially God's goodness, to be one of the most powerful weapons to combat evil.

---

[1] ROMANS 12:21.

In my Christian walk, I have found "the sword of the Spirit, which is the word of God" to be a most powerful weapon with which to fight the devil and his schemes.[2] I have tried to make Scripture memory a personal and family habit.[3] Having God's Word hidden in my heart and mind has proven invaluable. Being able to recall Scripture in times of need has provided comfort and guidance and given strength and peace.

In your battle to overcome evil with good, what are you doing to sharpen your "sword?" Like Spurgeon, I encourage you to memorize Scripture. May your grip upon "the sword of the Spirit" be so strong that you can proficiently wield and employ it in the daily battles you face. Like the mighty warrior, Eleazor, who held tightly to his sword, may you fight with such courage and valor that your hand is frozen to the hilt of God's Word.[4]

All Scripture is God-breathed and is useful for teaching, rebuking, correcting and training in righteousness, so the man of God may be thoroughly equipped for every good work.
—*2* TIMOTHY *3:16–17*

---

[2] EPHESIANS 6:17.

[3] When our children were young, we used SWORD FIGHTING by Karyn Henley as a daily devotional. Each week presented a new "Sword" for memory. I recommend it as a parental guide as you strive to hide God's Word in your children's hearts.

[4] 2 SAMUEL 23:9–10.

CHAPTER 44

SCRIPTURAL PRAYERS FOR DIFFICULT TIMES

Praise be to the God and Father of our Lord Jesus Christ, the Father of compassion and the God of all comfort, who comforts us in all our troubles, so that we can comfort those in any trouble with the comfort we ourselves receive from God. For just as the sufferings of Christ flow over into our lives, so also through Christ our comfort overflows. If we are distressed, it is for your comfort and salvation; if we are comforted, it is for your comfort, which produces in you patient endurance of the same sufferings we suffer. And our hope for you is firm, because we know that just as you share in our sufferings, so also you share in our comfort.
—2 CORINTHIANS 1:3–7

O Sovereign Lord, you are the One who sees and knows all things. You know the cares and concerns of our hearts, as well as the stress, strains, and fears _____ is encountering.

May _____ "trust in you at all times; pour out his/her heart to you; knowing God is a refuge" (PSALM 62:8).

Guard _____ spiritually, mentally, physically, emotionally, and socially. "Surround _____ with your favor as with a shield" (PSALM 5:12).

Please be _____ 's "shield and helper and glorious sword" (DEUTERONOMY 33:29).

Command your angels concerning _____ to guard him/her in all his/her ways (PSALM 91:11).

By the power of your Holy Spirit please "strengthen _____'s feeble hands, steady the knees that give away; speak to those with fearful hearts" (ISAIAH 35:4).

May _____ know "Your Word is truth" (JOHN 17:17).

By the power of your Holy Spirit help _____ trust in you. Your Word that says, "Be strong, do not fear, for I am with you; do not be dismayed, for I am your God. I will strengthen you and help you; I will uphold you with my righteous right hand" (ISAIAH 41:10).

Graciously "set your seal of ownership on _____ and put your Spirit in _____'s heart" (2 CORINTHIANS 1:20–22).

May the LORD give strength to his people! May the LORD bless his people with peace!
—(PSALM 29:11).

REFLECTION

When we get into difficult circumstances, we impoverish His ministry by saying, 'Of course, He can't do anything about this.' We struggle to reach the bottom of our own well, trying to get water for ourselves. Beware of sitting back, and saying, 'It can't be done.' You will know it can be done if you will look to Jesus. The well of your incompleteness runs deep, but make the effort to look away from yourself and to look toward Him.
—Oswald Chambers, MY UTMOST FOR HIS HIGHEST, FEBRUARY 27

In the midst of difficult circumstances, it takes conscientious effort to look away from our situation toward Jesus. During these times, our vision becomes myopic. Hyper-focused on the difficulty, we become crippled with fear, anxiety, and doubt. When we correct our gaze toward the Almighty, our anxieties are assuaged. Ruth, the daughter of the great evangelist Billy Graham, recounted a story which illustrates this well.

One day Ruth received a distressing call from her daughter who was having medical complications. She was told to come right away. Filled with anxiety and fear, Ruth hopped in the car. She knew she needed to pray, but the words would not come. She turned on the radio, hoping to find a Christian song or message of peace and comfort. None played. She knew she needed the Lord's help but could not even focus long enough to come up with a prayer.

After some time worrying, Ruth refocused her gaze. She took her eyes off the tenuous situation and turned them toward heaven. Recalling God's names, attributes, and his Word, her fears began to subside as she trusted in God and what he was able to do.

When I find myself in situations like Ruth Graham found herself, I turn to one of my favorite Bible verses, PSALM 105:4–5. "Look to the LORD and his strength; seek his face always. Remember the wonders he has done." As I seek the Lord's face, I recall his names, his love, and his faithfulness in keeping his promises. Peace and assurance comes over me and helps me cope with the present situation. My focus shifts from my situation to my Savior.

Beloved, during difficult times in your life, shift your gaze from your situation to your Savior. Do not worry when you are not able to put your sighs and groans into words. "The Holy Spirit takes part with us and makes our weak prayers effective."[1] Paul reminds us "the Holy Spirit helps us in our weakness," praying with and for us "in accordance with God's will."[2]

Regardless of the circumstance, Scripture instructs, "Humble yourselves, therefore under God's mighty hand, that he may lift you

---

[1] Wayne Grudem, SYSTEMATIC THEOLOGY, AN INTRODUCTION TO BIBLICAL DOCTRINE, (Zondervan 1994), 382.

[2] ROMANS 8:26–27.

up in due time. Cast your anxiety on him because he cares for you … And the God of all grace, who called you to his eternal glory in Christ, after you have suffered a little while, will himself restore you and make you strong, firm and steadfast. To him be the power for ever and ever. Amen."[3]

---

[3] 1 PETER 5:5–11.

CHAPTER 45

THE GREATEST COMMANDMENT

ADORATION

Praise the LORD.

I will extol the LORD with all my heart
in the council of the upright and in the assembly.

Great are the works of the Lord;
they are pondered by all who delight in them.
Glorious and majestic are his deeds,
and his righteousness endures forever.
He has caused his wonders to be remembered;
the LORD is gracious and compassionate.
He provides food for those who fear him;
he remembers his covenant forever.
He has shown his people the power of his works,
giving them the lands of other nations.
The works of his hands are faithful and just;
all his precepts are trustworthy.
They are steadfast forever and ever,
done in faithfulness and uprightness.
He provided redemption for his people;
he ordained his covenant forever—
holy and awesome is his name.

The fear of the LORD is the beginning of wisdom;
all who follow his precepts have good understanding.
To him belong eternal praise.
—PSALM 111

PAUSE AND ADORE HIM.

CONFESSION

Let us throw off everything that hinders and the sin that so easily entangles.
—HEBREWS 12:1

Put to death whatever belongs to our earthly nature: sexual immorality, impurity, lust, evil desires and greed, which is idolatry. Let us rid ourselves of anger, rage, malice, slander, and filthy language from our lips.
—COLOSSIANS 3:5–9

PAUSE AND CONFESS YOUR SINS.

THANKSGIVING

For as high as the heavens are above the earth, so great is his love for those who fear him; as far as the east is from the west, so far has he removed our transgressions from us.
—PSALM 103:11–12

We "thank you Father for qualifying us to share in the inheritance of the saints in the kingdom of light. We thank you for rescuing us from the dominion of darkness and bringing us into the kingdom of the Son you love, in whom we have redemption, the forgiveness of sins" (COLOSSIANS 1:12–13).

PAUSE AND THANK HIM.

SUPPLICATION

Lord God, I pray for _____ to "love you with all his/her heart, soul, strength and mind; and to love his/her neighbor as himself/herself" (DEUTERONOMY 6:5, MATTHEW 22:37–39).

May "your commandments be upon _____ 's heart" (DEUTERONOMY 6:6).

Keep your "Word very near _____; in _____ 's mouth and in his/her heart so that _____ may obey it" (Deuteronomy 30:14).

Reflection

Generally, love is thought of as an emotion born out of the heart and soul; a feeling, like when one "falls in love". Rarely does one think of love in terms of an intellectual pursuit. However, the Greatest Commandment calls us to love God with our minds.

A problem we encounter in loving God with our minds is, like the rest of our being, our minds were affected in the fall and have been corrupted by sin. "The noetic effects of sin describe the impact of sin upon the *nous* (the mind) of fallen humanity. The faculty of thinking, with which we reason, has been seriously disturbed and corrupted by the fall."[1] Romans 1:28 states the unregenerate mind "a depraved mind."

The unregenerate mind, once born again, becomes more favorably disposed to thinking of God. The sanctifying work of the Holy Spirit places in us desires to "set our minds on things above"[2] and pursue a knowledge and love of God with our minds.

Christian speaker, writer, and teacher Jen Wilkin said, "the heart cannot love what the mind does not know. Yes, it is sinful to acquire knowledge for knowledge's sake, but acquiring knowledge about One we love, for the sake of loving him more deeply, will always be for our transformation."[3] Therefore, the Bible emphasizes the importance of loving the Lord with "all your heart and all your mind."[4] Jen states, "We must love God with our minds, allowing our intellect to inform our emotions, rather than the other way around."

---

[1] R. C. Sproul, "Loving God with Our Minds," TableTalk, (June 2017), 4–5.

[2] Colossians 3:2.

[3] Jen Wilkin, Women of the Word, (Crossway, 2014), 33–34.

[4] Matthew 22:37; Mark 12:30; Luke 10:27.

Loving God with our minds entails deepening our biblical understanding of his nature, redemptive work, sovereignty, and providence. A deeper understanding of who God is and what he has done fuels emotive expressions of love for him, such as an emotional reaction during a hymn. This is the antithesis of loving God with our emotions only, which too often entails loving a "god" we fabricate, in part, to conform to our own sinful emotions, desires, and behavior.

Are you striving to love God with your mind? Are you allowing your intellect to inform your emotions rather than the other way around? R.C. Sproul said, "True Christians want God to dominate their thinking and to fill their minds with ideas of himself."[5] Is God dominating your thinking? Pray you will "be transformed by the renewing of your minds"[6] so you can know God's will, and love him more as you set your thoughts on him.

And this is my prayer: that your love may abound more and more in knowledge and depth of insight, so that you may be able to discern what is best and may be pure and blameless until the day of Christ, filled with the fruit of righteousness that comes through Jesus Christ – to the glory and praise of God.
—PHILIPPIANS 1:9–10

---

[5] R. C. Sproul, "Loving God with Our Minds," TABLETALK, (June 2017), 4–5.

[6] Romans 12:1–2

CHAPTER 46

The Golden Rule

Adoration

Praise God! He is good and upright.

> Good and upright is the Lord; therefore, he instructs sinners in his ways.
> —Psalm 25:8

> The Lord is upright; he is my Rock, and there is no wickedness in him.
> —Psalm 92:15

Praise God! He is loving, faithful, righteous, and just.

> Your love, O Lord, reaches to the heavens, your faithfulness to the skies. Your righteousness is like the mighty mountains, your justice like the great deep. O Lord, you preserve both man and beast. How priceless is your unfailing love!
> —Psalm 36:5–7

Praise God for his unfailing kindness.

> The Lord lives! Praise be to my Rock! Exalted be God, the Rock, my Savior! Therefore, I will praise you, O Lord, among the nations; I will sing praises to your name. He gives his king great victories; he shows unfailing kindness to his anointed.
> —2 Samuel 22:47, 50–51

Pause and adore him.

Confession

Father, forgive us. "We are an unbelieving and perverse generation" (Matthew 17:17).

Have mercy on me, O God, according to your unfailing love;
according to your great compassion blot out my transgressions.
Wash away all my iniquity and cleanse me from my sin.
—Psalm 51:1–2

Pause and confess your sins.

Thanksgiving

Father, we thank you that we can "draw near to God with a sincere heart in full assurance of faith, having our hearts sprinkled
to cleanse us from a guilty conscience and having our bodies
washed with pure water" (Hebrews 10:22).

Pause and thank him.

Supplication

Good and merciful God, I pray _____ will emulate your
love and kindness. In everything, may _____ "do to others
what _____ would have them do to him/her, for this sums
up the Law and the Prophets" (Matthew 7:12).

REFLECTION

Throughout the centuries, many different religions, cultures, and civilizations have lived by a moral code commonly known as the Golden Rule. The rule is called "golden" because there is value in treating others as you would like them to treat you.

When Jesus taught the Golden Rule on the Sermon on the Mount, he explained to his listeners that everything recorded in the Jewish law and all that the prophets had taught could be summed up in one rule. His teaching caught their ears because of the positive way he stated a general principle that had previously been taught in a negative form—avoid harming others in ways you would find hurtful. In other words, don't do to others what you don't want done to you.

Similarly, Jesus' New Testament teaching of the Greatest Commandment was based on a negatively stated Old Testament law, "Do not seek revenge or bear a grudge against one of your people, but love your neighbor as yourself."[1]

Follower of Jesus, are you living positively for Jesus? Live by the Greatest Commandment and the Golden Rule. Love your neighbor as yourself. "Do good to all people."[2] Extend mercy and grace toward others. "So in everything, do to others what you would have them do to you, for this sums up the Law and the Prophets."[3]

---

[1] LEVITICUS 19:18

[2] GALATIANS 6:10

[3] MATTHEW 7:12

CHAPTER 47

THE LORD'S PRAYER

ADORATION

Give ear to my words, O LORD, consider my sighing. Listen to my cry for help, my King and my God, for to you I pray. In the morning, O LORD, you hear my voice; in the morning I lay my requests before you and wait in expectation.
—PSALM 5:1–3

But I, by your great mercy, will come into your house; in reverence will I bow down toward your holy temple. Lead me, O LORD, in your righteousness because of my enemies—make straight your way before me.
—PSALM 5:7–8

Yours, LORD, is the greatness and the power and the glory and the majesty and the splendor, for everything in heaven and earth is yours. Yours, LORD, is the kingdom; you are exalted as head over all.
—1 CHRONICLES 29:11

PAUSE AND ADORE HIM.

CONFESSION

For if you forgive other people when they sin against you, your heavenly Father will also forgive you. But if you do not forgive others their sins, your Father will not forgive your sins.
—MATTHEW 6:14–15

You are not a God who takes pleasure in evil; with you the wicked cannot dwell. The arrogant cannot stand in your presence; you hate all who do wrong. You destroy those who tell lies; bloodthirsty and deceitful men the LORD abhors.
—PSALM 5:4–6

PAUSE AND CONFESS YOUR SINS.

THANKSGIVING

But let all who take refuge in you be glad; let them ever sing for joy. Spread your protection over them, that those who love your name may rejoice in you. For surely, O LORD, you bless the righteous; you surround them with your favor as with a shield. —PSALM 5:11–12

PAUSE AND THANK HIM.

SUPPLICATION

This, then, is how you should pray:

Our Father in heaven, may _____ hallow your name.
Prepare _____ for your kingdom to come, your will to be done, on earth as it in heaven.
Give _____ this day his/her daily bread.
May _____ seek forgiveness of his/her debts and forgive his/her debtors.
Lead _____ not into temptation but deliver _____ from the evil one.
May _____ know Yours is the kingdom and the power and the glory. Amen (MATTHEW 6:9–13, *The Lord's Prayer*).

REFLECTION

The Lord's Prayer is a prayer most of us can recite. The majority of the time, we rush through the Lord's Prayer without thought. I, for one, am guilty as charged.

Recorded in MATTHEW 6:5–13, Jesus teaches about prayer. In the five verses leading up to the Lord's Prayer, he uses the word *pray* five times. In these passages, Jesus also critiques the Pharisees' and

Gentiles' prayers before giving his disciples the model prayer. He condemned the showy, pious prayer of the Pharisees and the babblings of the Gentiles and warns, "Do not be like them." Then, he says, "This is how you should pray." What follows are six petitions, three related to God and three to mankind.

Starting with *Our Father in heaven, hallowed be your name*, the prayer acknowledges the personal relationship we can have with God by being able to call him our "Father". This first petition also acknowledges God's attributes of holiness, purity, and complete separation from sin. The focus is on God and who *he* is, not ourselves.

Praying *Thy kingdom come* is a petition for God to expand his kingdom on earth now as we wait for the "kingdom to come" when Christ reigns forever. This request is for the Lord to open one's heart and mind so he can be united with Christ as Savior and Lord and honor him as King now; for the gospel to spread so others will be saved.

Thy will be done refers to God's absolute rule over all things. It is a humble petition and desire for God's sovereign will to be done over ours. J. I. Packer said this petition is "not to make God do my will (which is practicing magic), but to bring my will into line with his (which is what it means to practice true religion)."[1]

After acknowledging God's immanence and transcendence, and his rule and reign as Sovereign Lord, the prayer transitions to man and acknowledges his creaturely dependence upon his Creator to provide daily for his every need. In utter dependence, requests are to be made daily for bread, for the forgiveness of sins, and for strength to overcome temptation and be delivered from evil. As Albert Mohler said, "The Lord's Prayer clearly expresses the glory of God and the gospel of grace. It reveals the coming of the kingdom of Christ, the forgiveness provided by the King, his daily provision and care for his people, and his deliverance of his people from the powers of this age."[2]

For years I have prayed this model prayer, and not until recently did I notice the omission of "thanksgiving." Why was thanksgiving

---

[1] J. I. Packer, GROWING IN CHRIST, (Crossway Books, 1994), 179.

[2] R. Albert Mohler, Jr., THE PRAYER THAT TURNS THE WORLD UPSIDE DOWN, (Nelson Books, 2018), 168.

omitted when Scripture clearly teaches us to "give thanks?"[3] Jesus himself gave thanks to God for hearing his prayers[4] and for his provision.[5] Why not here?

Though not explicit, thanksgiving is implicit. For when we come to God the Father with our hearts and minds, we cannot help but acknowledge that God is our Supreme Ruler, Provider, Redeemer, and Deliverer and respond with effusive praise and thanksgiving.

Reflecting on this prayer has caused my prayer to be: *Father, may I never again open my mouth and mindlessly repeat The Lord's Prayer, but think about the words you taught me to pray. May my words give full expression to the glory, honor, praise, and thanksgiving due your holy name for all that you have done and will do now, and in the kingdom to come. Amen.*

Recommended reading:

THE PRAYER THAT TURNS THE WORLD UPSIDE DOWN: THE LORD'S PRAYER AS A MANIFESTO FOR REVOLUTION by R. Albert Mohler, Jr., Nelson Books, 2018.

---

[3] 1 THESSALONIANS 5:18; 1 CHRONICLES 16:34, 35; PSALM 7:17; PSALM 118.

[4] JOHN 11:41.

[5] MATTHEW 14:16–21; 15:35–38; 26:26–27.

CHAPTER 48

SALVATION

ADORATION

Praise God! He is our strength, our song, our salvation—our Savior!

I, I am the LORD, and besides me there is no savior.
—ISAIAH 43:11 ESV

This is the name by which he will be called: The LORD Our Righteous Savior.
—JEREMIAH 23:6

The LORD is my strength and song; he has become my salvation. He is my God, and I will praise him.
—EXODUS 15:2

The LORD lives! Praise be to my Rock! Exalted be God, the Rock, my Savior.
—2 SAMUEL 22:47

The LORD is my rock, my fortress and my deliver; my God is my rock, in whom I take refuge, my shield and the horn of my salvation. He is my stronghold, my refuge and my savior.
—2 SAMUEL 22:2–3

He alone is my rock and my salvation; he is my fortress, I will never be shaken.
—PSALM 62:2

The LORD is the strength of his people, a fortress of salvation for his anointed one.
—PSALM 28:8

Salvation belongs to our God, who sits on the throne, and to the Lamb. Praise and glory and wisdom and thanks and honor and power and strength be to our God for ever and ever. Amen!
—REVELATION 7:10, 12

PAUSE AND ADORE HIM.

CONFESSION

If my people, who are called by my name, will humble themselves and pray and seek my face and turn from their wicked ways, then will I hear from heaven and will forgive their sin and will heal their land.
—2 CHRONICLES 7:14

Therefore, confess your sins to each other and pray for each other so that you may be healed.
—JAMES 5:16

PAUSE AND CONFESS YOUR SINS.

THANKSGIVING

Praise be to the LORD, to God our Savior, who daily bears our burdens.
—PSALM 68:19

My soul will rejoice in the LORD and delight in his salvation.
—PSALM 35:9

Therefore, I will "joyfully give thanks to the Father, who has qualified you to share in the inheritance of the saints in the kingdom of light."
—COLOSSIANS 1:12

Thanks be to God! He gives us the victory through our Lord Jesus Christ.
—1 CORINTHIANS 15:57

PAUSE AND THANK HIM.

Supplication

I pray to you, O Lord, in the time of your favor; in your great love, O God, answer me with your sure salvation (Psalm 69:13).

My heart's desire and prayer is that _____ be saved (Romans 10:1–2).

Your Word states you do "not want anyone to perish, but everyone to come to repentance" (2 Peter 3:9).

I pray _____ may "obtain the salvation that is in Christ Jesus, with eternal glory" (2 Timothy 2:10).

May _____ realize "now is the time of God's favor, now is the day of salvation" (2 Corinthians 6:2).

May _____ believe that "God so loved the world that He gave His one and only Son, that whoever believes in Him shall not perish but have everlasting life"(John 3:16).

By the power of your Holy Spirit, "fill _____ with the knowledge of your will through all spiritual wisdom and understanding. May _____ live a life worthy of the Lord and please him in every way" (Colossians 1:9–10).

Pray for those who need salvation.

REFLECTION

> *For by grace you have been saved, through faith—and this*
> *not from yourselves, it is the gift of God—not by works, so*
> *that no one can boast.*
> —EPHESIANS 2:8–9

In 3 JOHN 4, the apostle John states, "I have no greater joy than to hear that my children are walking in the truth." For years I have heard parents quote this verse and believed it referred to physical children. It was not until recently that I read the verse in context and realized it refers to spiritual children, to those whom John was discipling, for whom he was a spiritual father.

When Jesus gives the Great Commission in MATTHEW 28 to "go and make disciples," he is telling his followers to become spiritual fathers to those he puts in their path. His desire is for his disciples to make disciples.

For some, spreading the Good News is easy. To others, evangelism is a daunting task. I personally have found the ABC's an easy way to share God's free gift of salvation. May you find the guide and prayer below helpful as you share with others that salvation is found in Jesus Christ alone.

A—Admit to God you are a sinner and ask for God's forgiveness of your sins.

> For all have sinned and fall short of the glory of God.
> —ROMANS 3:23

> There is no one righteous, not even one.
> —ROMANS 3:10

B—Believe Jesus Christ, the Righteous One, is the atoning sacrifice for your sins.

> For God so loved the world that he gave his only Son, that whoever believes in him shall not perish but have eternal life.
> —JOHN 3:16

> This is how God showed his love among us: He sent his one and only Son into the world that we might live through him. This is love: not that we loved God, but that he loved us and sent his Son as an atoning sacrifice for our sins.
> —1 JOHN 4:10

> Believe in the Lord Jesus, and you will be saved.
> —ACTS 16:31

C—Confess Christ as Lord.

> If you confess with your mouth that "Jesus is Lord," and believe in your heart that God raised him from the dead, you will be saved. For it is with your heart that you believe and are justified, and it is with our mouth that you confess and are saved.
> —ROMANS 10:9–10

Father in heaven, I humbly come before your throne of grace and admit I have fallen short of your holy and righteous standard. I have sinned in thought, word, and deed. I have committed sins of commission and omission. Please forgive every way I have transgressed your law.

God, I know you are a just God and believe you gave Jesus Christ as an atoning sacrifice for my sins; that Christ's shed blood on the cross cleanses me from all unrighteousness. I confess Jesus as Lord of my life and trust in his righteousness alone for salvation.

Thank you for loving me and extending your grace, mercy, and forgiveness toward me. I know it is by grace alone, through faith alone, and in Christ's righteousness alone that I am saved.

Now, Lord, be pleased to clothe me in your righteousness, so I may stand faultless before your throne. Please fill me with the Holy Spirit so I may walk in newness of life, with a desire to obey your commands, and live a life that is pleasing to you. In the name of Jesus, my Lord and Savior, I pray. Amen.

There is rejoicing in the presence of the angels of God over one sinner who repents.
—Luke 15:10

SECTION V

PRAYERS FOR THE HOLIDAYS

CHAPTER 49

NEW YEAR

ADORATION

Praise be to the God and Father of our Lord Jesus Christ! In his great mercy he has given us new birth into a living hope through the resurrection of Jesus Christ from the dead, and into an inheritance that can never perish, spoil or fade—kept in heaven for you, who through faith are shielded by God's power until the coming of the salvation that is ready to be revealed in the last time.
—1 PETER 1:3–5

I will praise you, O LORD, with all my heart; I will tell of all your wonders. I will be glad and rejoice in you; I will sing praise to your name, O Most High ... Sing praises to the LORD, enthroned in Zion; proclaim among the nations what he has done.
—PSALM 9:1–2, 11

Sing to the LORD a new song, for he has done marvelous things; his right hand and his holy arm have worked salvation for him.
—PSALM 98:1

"I am making everything new!" Then he said, "Write this down, for these words are trustworthy and true."
—REVELATION 21:5

PAUSE AND PRAY.

CONFESSION

Father, forgive us! How often we "gratify the desires of the flesh" (GALATIANS 5:16).

The acts of the sinful nature are obvious: sexual immorality, impurity and debauchery; idolatry and witchcraft; hatred, discord, jealousy, fits of rage, selfish ambition, dissensions, factions and envy; drunkenness, orgies, and the like.
—GALATIANS 5:19–21

Help me Lord to live by the Spirit and put to death the misdeeds of the body, so I may live (ROMANS 8:12–13).

PAUSE AND CONFESS YOUR SINS.

THANKSGIVING

Therefore, if anyone is in Christ, he is a new creation; the old has gone, the new has come! All this is from God, who reconciled us to himself through Christ and gave us the ministry of reconciliation: that God was reconciling the world to himself in Christ, not counting men's sins against them. And he has committed to us the message of reconciliation. We are therefore Christ's ambassadors, as though God were making his appeal through us. We implore you on Christ's behalf: Be reconciled to God. God made him who had no sin to be sin for us, so that in him we might become the righteousness of God.
—2 CORINTHIANS 5:17–21

PAUSE AND THANK HIM.

SUPPLICATION

Sovereign LORD, I pray you will "give _____ an undivided heart and put a new spirit in him/her. By the power of your Holy Spirit remove from _____ his/her heart of stone and give _____ a heart of flesh. May _____ follow your decrees and be careful to keep your law. May _____ be yours and you be _____ 's God" (EZEKIEL 11:18–20).

"Put a new song in _____ 's mouth, a hymn of praise to God." This New Year may "many see and fear and put their trust in the LORD" (PSALM 40:3).

REFLECTION

As well-intended as the tradition may be, New Year's resolutions generally fizzle before the sparklers go out. Personal promises to eat better, exercise more, lose weight, save more, spend less, or quit a bad habit generally go up in smoke before the month's end. Spiritual resolutions to pray more, sin less, read the Bible daily, be active in church or Bible study generally fall by the wayside as well. We generally strive with our own power and might. If we were truthful with ourselves, we would admit we often make resolutions without giving much deference to God.

The Bible tells us, "Seek first the kingdom of God and his righteousness, and all these things will be given to you as well."[1] Our highest priority every day should be a right relationship with God, seeking his desires for our lives. We should ask the Lord to impress upon our hearts what he wants us to do this day, this year, knowing that he promises to "supply all our needs according to His glorious riches in Christ Jesus."[2]

Consider starting the New Year on your knees. Humbly seek the Lord in prayer.

You were taught, with regard to your former way of life, to put off your old self, which is being corrupted by its deceitful desires; to be made new in the attitude of your minds; and to put on the new self, created to be like God in true righteousness and holiness.
—EPHESIANS 4:22–24

Pray. Ask God for wisdom regarding what sort of resolutions you should make. Will it make you more righteous and holy?

---

[1] MATTHEW 6:33.

[2] PHILIPPIANS 4:19.

Trust. Rely upon God to direct your thoughts. Ask God to give you someone to hold you accountable. He will supply all your needs.[3] When you fall, look to the Lord and have confidence knowing he will renew the strength of those who hope in him.[4]

Remember, "Physical training is of some value, but godliness has value for all things, holding promise for both the present life and the life to come."[5]

Finally, be strong in the Lord and in his mighty power. Put on the full armor of God so that you can take your stand against the devil's schemes... In addition to all this, take up the shield of faith with which you can extinguish all the flaming arrows of the evil one. Take the helmet of salvation and the sword of the Spirit, which is the word of God. And pray in the Spirit on all occasions with all kinds of prayers and requests. With this in mind, be alert and always keep on praying for all the saints.
—EPHESIANS 6:10–11, 16–18

---

[3] PHILIPPIANS 4:19.

[4] ISAIAH 40:31.

[5] 1 TIMOTHY 4:8.

CHAPTER 50

EASTER

Christ has risen! He has risen indeed!

ADORATION

He is not here; he has risen, just as he said.
—MATTHEW 28:6

He has risen! He is not here!
—MARK 16:6

He is not here; He has risen!
—LUKE 24:6

For what I received I passed on to you as of first importance: that Christ died for our sins according to the Scriptures, that he was buried, that he was raised on the third day according to the Scriptures.
—1 CORINTHIANS 15:3–4

They killed him by hanging him on a tree, but God raised him from the dead on the third day and caused him to be seen. He commanded us to preach to the people and to testify that he is the one whom God appointed as judge of the living and the dead. All the prophets testify about him that everyone who believes in him receives forgiveness of sins through his name.
—ACTS 10:39–40, 42–44

Behold, the Lamb of God, who takes away the sin of the world!
—JOHN 1:29

Worthy is the Lamb, who was slain, to receive power and wealth and wisdom and strength and honor and glory and praise!
—REVELATION 5:12

Salvation belongs to our God who sits on the throne, and to the Lamb!
—REVELATION 7:10

Blessing and glory and wisdom and thanksgiving and honor and power and might be to our God forever and ever! Amen.
—REVELATION 7:12

PAUSE AND ADORE HIM.

CONFESSION

Read ISAIAH 59

Surely the arm of the LORD is not too short to save, nor his ear too dull to hear. But your iniquities have separated you from your God; your sins have hidden his face from you, so that he will not hear. For your hands are stained with blood, your fingers with guilt. Your lips have spoken lies, your tongues muttered wicked things.
—ISAIAH 59:1–3

PAUSE AND CONFESS YOUR SINS.

THANKSGIVING

We all, like sheep, have gone astray, each of us has turned to his own way; and the LORD has laid on him the iniquity of us all.
—ISAIAH 53:6

You were ransomed from the futile ways inherited from your forefathers, not with perishable things such as silver or gold, but with the precious blood of Christ, like that of a lamb without blemish or spot.
—1 PETER 1:18–19

For Christ died for sins once for all, the righteous for the unrighteous, to bring you to God.
—1 PETER 3:18

Because he poured out his soul to death and was numbered with the transgressors; yet he bore the sin of many, and makes intercession for the transgressors.
—ISAIAH 53:12 ESV

But he was pierced for our transgressions; he was crushed for our iniquities; upon him was the chastisement that brought us peace, and with his wounds we are healed.
—ISAIAH 53:5 ESV

For there is one God, and there is one mediator between God and men, the man Christ Jesus, who gave himself as a ransom for all.
—1 TIMOTHY 2:5 ESV

But thanks be to God! He gives us the victory through our Lord Jesus Christ.
—1 CORINTHIANS 15:57

PAUSE AND THANK HIM.

SUPPLICATION

Lamb of God, your Word says, "the message of the cross is foolishness to those who are perishing, but to us who are being saved it is the power of God" (1 CORINTHIANS 1:18).

God our Savior wants all men to be saved and to come to a knowledge of the truth (1 TIMOTHY 2:3–4).

Lord, you are "patient with us, not wanting any to perish, but everyone to come to repentance" (2 PETER 3:9).

"God pour out your love into _____'s heart by the power of the Holy Spirit" (ROMANS 5:5).

"Open _____'s mind so that he/she can understand the Scriptures" (LUKE 24:45).

May _____ know "if he/she confesses with his/her mouth that Jesus is Lord and believes in his/her heart that God raised Christ from the dead, he/she will be saved" (ROMANS 10:9).

REFLECTION

> *Look to the cross and see "that lonely, twisted, tortured figure on the cross, nails through hands and feet, back lacerated, limbs wrenched, brow bleeding from thorn-pricks, mouth dry and intolerably thirsty, plunged in God-forsaken darkness. This is the God for me! He laid aside his immunity to pain. He entered our world of flesh and blood, tears and death. He suffered for us."*
> —John Stott, THE CROSS OF CHRIST, IVP Books, 2006.

Even though Henry Wadsworth Longfellow lived long before my time, I think he had me in mind when he penned, "There Was A Little Girl." Like the little girl in his poem, *"When I was good, I was very good indeed, But when I was bad, I was horrid."* A story from my childhood, recounted by my mother, illustrates this point well.

One night, as was her practice, my devoted mother knelt beside my bed to pray. Being Easter eve, she shared the story of Christ's life, death, and resurrection[1], adding that "his Spirit now lives everywhere."[2] In my sinful, childish mind, it bothered me that God's Spirit was everywhere. I saw him as an unwanted intruder who had invaded my space. Disturbed, I responded, "You get from under these covers, you Jesus you, and don't think you're getting any of my Easter eggs either!" Flabbergasted at my response, my mother tried to further reason, but to no avail.

---

[1] 1 CORINTHIANS 15:1, 3–5.

[2] PSALM 139:7–10.

At the time, I was dead in my sins[3] and did not understand the gospel. "For the message of the cross is foolishness to those who are perishing, but to us who are being saved it is the power of God."[4] Even though it was years before I understood the powerful message of the cross, my mother was fulfilling her duty as a Christian parent to share the gospel.

After Christ's death, burial, and resurrection, he returned to give his disciples a parting command, "Go and make disciples."[5] This imperative is for us as well. Like my mother, we are to share the good news that "Christ died for sins once for all, the righteous for the unrighteous to bring you to God. He was put to death in the body but made alive by the Spirit."[6] It is our Christian duty to share the gospel; it is Christ's work to save.[7] This Easter, pray for opportunities to share the gospel. Proclaim with all the saints, "He has risen indeed!"

---

[3] COLOSSIANS 2:13.

[4] 1 CORINTHIANS 1:18.

[5] MATTHEW 28:19.

[6] 1 PETER 3:18.

[7] EPHESIANS 2:8–9.

CHAPTER 51

THANKSGIVING

ADORATION

Give thanks to the LORD, call on his name; make known among the nations what he has done. Sing to him, sing praise to him; tell of all his wonderful acts. Glory in his holy name; let the hearts of those who seek the LORD rejoice. Look to the LORD and his strength; seek his face always.
—PSALM 105:1–4

Give thanks to the LORD, for he is good. His love endures forever. Give thanks to the God of gods. His love endures forever. Give thanks to the LORD of lords. His love endures forever. Give thanks to the God of heaven. His love endures forever. Give thanks to him who alone does great wonders, who by his understanding made the heavens, who spread out the earth upon the waters, who made the great lights—the sun to govern the day, the moon and stars to govern the night, to the One who remembered us in our low estate and freed us from our enemies, and who gives food to every creature. Give thanks to the LORD Almighty, for the LORD is good; his love endures forever.
—Select verses from PSALM 136

We give thanks to you, O God, we give thanks for your Name is near; men tell of your wonderful deeds.
—PSALM 75:1

Enter his gates with thanksgiving and his courts with praise; give thanks to him and praise his name. For the LORD is good and his love endures forever; his faithfulness continues through all generations.
—PSALM 100:4–5

Give thanks to the LORD, for he is good; his love endures forever. Let the redeemed of the LORD say this... Let them give thanks to the LORD for his unfailing love and his wonderful deeds for men. Let them sacrifice thank offerings and tell of his works with songs of joy.
—PSALM 107:1–2, 21–22

Give thanks to the LORD, for he is good.
—PSALM 136:1

Give thanks to the God of gods.
—PSALM 136:2

Give thanks to the LORD of lords.
—PSALM 136:3

Give thanks to the God of heaven.
—PSALM 136:26

Give thanks to the LORD Almighty, for the Lord is good; his love endures forever.
—JEREMIAH 33:11

PAUSE AND ADORE HIM.

CONFESSION

We have sinned, even as our fathers did; we have done wrong and acted wickedly...we have given no thought to your miracles; we have not remembered your many kindnesses; we have not waited on your counsel; we have grumbled and disobeyed; for we have rebelled against the Spirit of God. Save us, O LORD, and gather us that we may give thanks to your holy name and glory in your praise.
—Select verses from PSALM 106

PAUSE AND CONFESS YOUR SINS.

THANKSGIVING

But thanks be to God, who always leads us as captives in Christ's triumphal procession and uses us to spread the aroma of the knowledge of him everywhere.
—2 CORINTHIANS 2:14

PAUSE AND THANK HIM.

SUPPLICATION

Gracious and merciful God, may "the peace of Christ rule in _____'s heart, and may _____ be thankful. Let the word of Christ dwell in _____ richly, and whatever _____ does, whether in word or deed, may he/she do it all in the name of the Lord Jesus, giving thanks to God the Father through him" (COLOSSIANS 3:15–17).

REFLECTION

One of the fundamental qualities invariably found in grateful persons is humility. Gratitude is the overflow of a humble heart, just as surely as an ungrateful, complaining spirit flows out of a proud heart.[1]
—Nancy Leigh DeMoss CHOOSING GRATITUDE

They were naked and unafraid, with literally everything in the world one could possibly want or need. It was all there for the taking, without even working for it. God had provided the perfect company, perfect food, perfect weather; everything in the Garden of Eden was perfect. Peace and harmony prevailed. There was

---

[1] Nancy Leigh DeMoss, CHOOSING GRATITUDE, (Moody Publishers, 2009), 183.

oneness with God, with creation, and with each other, until the crafty serpent arrived.[2]

Empty-handed, but mouth full of lies, the serpent came with a question. He prefaced his question with, *"Did God really say... "*[3] words meant to stir doubt. What was God withholding? And Why? Instead of humbly coming before the Lord with humble grateful hearts, Adam and Eve began to question God. They became discontented. Pride made them think they knew better than the One who made and had provided all their needs. They focused on the one thing they were forbidden, rather than all they had been graciously given.

Do you have a proud, ungrateful heart? Do you think you know better than the One who made you? Do you complain about what you do not have rather focus on all the blessings the Lord has given you? Rather than fixating on the "one thing" like Adam and Eve, choose gratitude and "give thanks to the Lord for his unfailing love and his wonderful deeds for men."[4]

Be joyful always; pray continually; give thanks in all circumstances, for this is God's will for you in Christ Jesus.
—1 THESSALONIANS 5:16–18

---

[2] GENESIS 2–3.

[3] GENESIS 3:1.

[4] PSALM 107:8.

CHAPTER 52

CHRISTMAS

ADORATION

Therefore, the Lord himself will give you a sign: The virgin will be with child and will give birth to a son and will call him Immanuel.
—ISAIAH 7:14

Glory to God in the highest, and on earth peace to men on whom his favor rests.
—LUKE 2:14

For to us a child is born, to us a son is given, and the government will be on his shoulders. And he will be called Wonderful Counselor, Mighty God, Everlasting Father, Prince of Peace.
—ISAIAH 9:6

She will give birth to a son, and you are to give him the name Jesus, because he will save his people from their sins… and they will call him Immanuel- which means, "God with us."
—MATTHEW 1:21, 23

He will be great and will be called the Son of the Most High.
—LUKE 1:32

My soul glorifies the Lord and my spirit rejoices in God my Savior.
—LUKE 1:46–47

PAUSE AND ADORE HIM.

CONFESSION

Do not love the world or anything in the world. If anyone loves the world, the love of the Father is not in him. For everything in the world—the cravings of sinful man, the lust of his eyes and the boasting of what he has and does—comes not from the Father but from the world. The world and its desires pass away, but the man who does the will of God lives forever.
—1 JOHN 2:15–17

PAUSE AND CONFESS YOUR SINS.

THANKSGIVING

Praise be to the Lord, the God of Israel, because he has come and has redeemed his people.
—LUKE 1:68

He is the atoning sacrifice for our sins, and not only for ours but also for the sins of the whole world.
—1 JOHN 2:2

Thanks be to God for His indescribable gift!
—2 CORINTHIANS 9:15

Every good and perfect gift is from above, coming down from the Father of the heavenly lights, who does not change like shifting shadows. He chose to give us birth through the word of truth, that we might be a kind of first fruits of all he created.
—JAMES 1:17–18

PAUSE AND THANK HIM.

SUPPLICATION

Father of heavenly lights, during this season of giving and receiving, may _____ receive your good and perfect gift of salvation through your Son Jesus Christ (JAMES 1:17; 1 THESSALONIANS 5:9).

Fill _____ with your Holy Spirit so that _____ "may understand what God has freely given" (1 CORINTHIANS 2:12).

I call upon you, Immanuel to dwell in _____ richly (MATTHEW 1:23).

Son of the Most High, you "did not come to be served, but to serve, and to give your life as a ransom for many" (MATTHEW 20:28).

May _____ be mindful of serving and giving, and not forget to "do good and to share with others, for with such sacrifice God is pleased" (HEBREWS 13:16).

REFLECTION

Lights! Camera! Action! Gifts! To many, that's what Christmas is—setting the stage for a production, where the focus is on the trimmings, forgetting the most important and significant part, the Gift!

Many years ago, to help my family focus on the reason for the season, my sister gave me a unique Christmas present. It was a golden wooden box topped with a silver bow. Inside were eight items. These items represent what was offered by our loving Heavenly Father to mankind that first Christmas—the underserved gift of salvation through his Son, Jesus Christ.[1] The box contains symbols of God's love gift:

---

[1] ROMANS 5:8; MATTHEW 7:11.

The broken chain represents how from the day of our conception[2] our lives have been swaddled in sin. Therefore, we need to "throw off everything that hinders and the sin that so easily entangles"[3] and run to the cross for forgiveness.

The perfectly plain note pad represents the fact that once "we confess our sins, God purifies us from all unrighteousness."[4] He wipes our slate clean.[5]

The white dove represents "the Spirit of God that descended like a dove"[6] and gives peace.[7]

The jingle bells represent the joy of the Lord that fills our soul and gives us strength as a result of receiving Christ as our Savior.[8]

The golden ring represents eternal life given to us in his Son.[9]

The Bible is a reminder to "let the word of Christ dwell in you richly so we can teach" others what God has offered through his Son.[10]

The key unlocks the treasure. "The fear of the Lord is the key to this treasure."[11]

The wooden cross inside a golden cup represents "the cup of the new covenant, Christ's blood, which was poured out for you on the cross."[12]

---

[2] Psalm 51:5.

[3] Hebrews 12:1–3.

[4] 1 John 1:9.

[5] Psalm 130:3.

[6] Matthew 3:16.

[7] Romans 15:13; Galatians 5:22; 1 Thessalonians 5:23.

[8] Nehemiah 8:10; Romans 15:13; Galatians 5:22.

[9] 1 John 5:11.

[10] Colossians 3:16.

[11] Isaiah 33:6.

[12] Luke 22:20.

Each Christmas, with a grateful heart, I pull out the golden box and place it under our tree. The box reminds me to focus on God's good and perfect gift, Jesus, and not get wrapped up in all the temporal gifts. Like my sister's present, pray for opportunities to share with others the one gift that will never spoil or fade,[13] God's gift of Immanuel.

Jesus is the best Christmas present ever!

---

[13] 1 PETER 1:4.

BENEDICTION

When Solomon had finished all these prayers and supplications to the LORD, he rose from before the altar of the LORD, where he had been kneeling with his hands spread out toward heaven. He stood and blessed the whole assembly of Israel in a loud voice, saying:

Praise be to the LORD, who has given rest to his people Israel just as he promised. Not one word has failed of all the good promises he gave through his servant Moses. May the LORD our God be with us as he was with our fathers; may he never leave us nor forsake us. May he turn our hearts to him; to walk in all his ways and keep the commands, decrees and regulations he gave our fathers. And may these words of mine, which I have prayed before the LORD, be near to the LORD our God day and night, that he may uphold the cause of his servant and the cause of his people Israel according to each day's need, so that all the peoples of the earth may know that the LORD is God and that there is no other. But your hearts must be fully committed to the LORD our God, to live by his decrees and obey his commands, as at this time.
—1 KINGS 8:54–61

May the grace of Christ our Savior
and the Father's boundless love,
with the Holy Spirit's favor,
rest upon us from above.

Thus, may we abide in union
with each other and the Lord,
and possess, in sweet communion,
joys which earth cannot afford.[1]

---

[1] John Newton, "May the Grace of Christ Our Savior," 1779.

BIBLIOGRAPHY

Begg, Alistair & Ferguson, Sinclair B. NAME ABOVE ALL NAMES. Wheaton: Crossway, 2013.

Bridges, Jerry. THE PRACTICE OF GODLINESS. Colorado Springs: NavPress, 1996.

Chambers, Oswald. MY UTMOST FOR HIS HIGHEST. Nashville: Discovery House (Thomas Nelson Publishers), 2005.

DeMoss, Nancy Leigh. CHOOSING GRATITUDE. Chicago: Moody Publishers, 2009.

Grudem, Wayne. SYSTEMATIC THEOLOGY: AN INTRODUCTION TO BIBLICAL DOCTRINE. Grand Rapids: Zondervan, 1994.

Hodge, A. A. OUTLINES OF THEOLOGY. Edinburgh: Banner of Truth, 1972.

Keller, Tim. COUNTERFEIT GODS: THE EMPTY PROMISES OF MONEY, SEX, AND POWER, AND THE ONLY HOPE THAT MATTERS. New York: Penguin, 2009.

Kipling, Rudyard and Fletcher, C. R. L. A SCHOOL HISTORY OF ENGLAND. London: Clarendon Press, 1911.

Lewis, C. S. MERE CHRISTIANITY. New York: Macmillan Publishers (Harper Collins Publishers), 1952.

Lloyd-Jones, Dr. Martyn. VINDICATION OF GOD. Banner of Truth, 1990.

Mohler, R. Albert, Jr. The Prayer that Turns the World Upside Down. Nashville: Nelson Books, 2018.

New Bible Commentary. Downers Grove: InterVarsity Press, 2010.

New Bible Dictionary Third Edition. Downers Grove: InterVarsity Press, 1996.

Palmer, B.M. Theology of Prayer. Richmond: Presbyterian Committee of Publication, 1894.

Packer, J. I. Growing In Christ. Wheaton: Crossway Books, 1994.

Piper, John. Desiring God: Meditations of a Christian Hedonist. Portland: Multnomah, 1986.

Stott, John. The Cross of Christ. Downers Grove: InterVarsity Press, 2006.

Swindoll, Chuck. The Grace Awakening. Nashville: Thomas Nelson, 2012.

TableTalk (magazine). Ligonier Ministries. Sanford, FL.

Teems, David. To Love Is Christ. Nashville: Thomas Nelson/Harper Collins, 2005.

Thomas, Derek W. H. Strength for the Weary. Sanford: Reformation Trust Publishing (Ligonier), 2018.

Wax, Trevin. The Gospel Coalition (periodical), "Counterfeit Gods: Tim Keller Takes On Our Idols." October 13, 2009.

Wilkin, Jen. Women of the Word. Wheaton: Crossway, 2014.

CPSIA information can be obtained
at www.ICGtesting.com
Printed in the USA
LVHW082051221120
672399LV00054B/2677